THE FOLGER LIBRARY
SHAKESPEARE

Designed to make Shakespeare's classic plays available to the general reader, each edition contains a reliable text with modernized spelling and punctuation,
scene-by-scene plot summaries, and explanatory
notes clarifying obscure and obsolete expressions.
An interpretive essay and accounts of Shakespeare's
life and theater form an instructive preface to each
play.

Louis B. Wright, General Editor, was the Director
of the Folger Shakespeare Library from 1948 until
his retirement in 1968. He is the author of *Middle-
Class Culture in Elizabethan England, Religion and
Empire, Shakespeare for Everyman,* and many other
books and essays on the history and literature of the
Tudor and Stuart periods.

Virginia Lamar, Assistant Editor, served as research
assistant to the Director and Executive Secretary of
the Folger Shakespeare Library from 1946 until her
death in 1968. She is the author of *English Dress in
the Age of Shakespeare* and *Travel and Roads in
England,* and coeditor of William Strachey's *Historie
of Travell into Virginia Britania.*

The Folger Shakespeare Library

GENERAL EDITOR

LOUIS B. WRIGHT

Director, Folger Shakespeare Library, 1948–1968

ASSISTANT EDITOR

VIRGINIA A. LaMAR

Executive Secretary, Folger Shakespeare Library, 1946–1968

The Folger Library General Reader's Shakespeare

THE HISTORY OF
HENRY
THE FOURTH
[PART 2]

By

WILLIAM
SHAKESPEARE

PUBLISHED BY POCKET BOOKS NEW YORK

POCKET BOOKS, a Simon & Schuster division of
GULF & WESTERN CORPORATION
1230 Avenue of the Americas, New York, N.Y. 10020

ISBN: 0-671-82594-1

First Pocket Books printing March, 1961

8th printing

Trademarks registered in the United States and other countries.

Printed in the U.S.A.

Preface

This edition of *Henry IV, Part 2*, is designed to make available a readable text of one of Shakespeare's greatest plays. In the centuries since Shakespeare many changes have occurred in the meanings of words, and some clarification of Shakespeare's vocabulary may be helpful. To provide the reader with necessary notes in the most accessible format, we have placed them on the pages facing the text that they explain. We have tried to make these notes as brief and simple as possible. Preliminary to the text we have also included a brief statement of essential information about Shakespeare and his stage. Readers desiring more detailed information should refer to the books suggested in the references, and if still further information is needed, the bibliographies in those books will provide the necessary clues to the literature of the subject.

L. B. W.
V. A. L.

September 1, 1960

Sequel to a Dramatic Success

Henry IV, Part 1 had enjoyed such a success upon the stage that Shakespeare would have been a foolish playwright indeed not to follow it up with a second play exploiting the same material. He probably planned it that way from the beginning because there is good reason to believe that he wanted to portray the whole sweep of history beginning with Richard II and culminating in the glorious reign of Henry V. Whether he originally planned a trilogy or a tetralogy no one can say, but the reception of the first play on Henry IV dictated a second part, which followed, perhaps fairly early in 1598.

As in the first part, Shakespeare alternates his scenes of history and comedy, but unlike some of the earlier playwrights, Shakespeare weaves together the comic and serious to achieve a greater unity than was characteristic of many Elizabethan plays, which often had comic subplots almost completely divorced from any connection with the main action. Falstaff is an officer engaged in the wars that involve the serious characters and he serves as foil and contrast. In fact, without Falstaff and his reprobate crew, who had been the boon companions of Prince Hal in his unregenerate youth, the King's worries over the Prince's conduct and the

Prince's later repentance and reform would have had much less dramatic effectiveness. One of Shakespeare's important contributions to the dramaturgy of his day was the example he gave of the organic use of the sub-plot, without which few plays could hope to hold the attention of the groundlings.

When the Quarto version of *The Second Part of Henry the Fourth* was published in 1600, the title page emphasized that the reader would be entertained "With the humors of Sir John Falstaff and swaggering Pistol." Pistol, the blustering (and cowardly) ensign, was a new comic character who had evidently made a greater hit on the stage than the passages in the preserved text would indicate, and hence the mention of his name in the title would help sell the play. The other comic parts were already familiar. Falstaff in Part 2 is still the quick-witted fat man who had endeared himself to the audience, but Shakespeare is already preparing for the time when Prince Hal must jettison his old play-fellow. Although the comic scenes are even more nu-merous than in Part 1, the Prince appears with Falstaff only once before the scene in which he rejects him, and then in a harmless prank in which he pokes fun at him. Without the Prince to serve as the inspiration of his wit, Falstaff is somewhat less spontaneous and a bit more labored than in the earlier play, but neverthe-less he remains an amusing old rascal, though hardly more than that. In Part 1 his villainy was that of a sharp-witted but boozy and bloated Robin Hood, but in Part 2 he has descended to chiseling Mistress Quickly and beating his board bill. The tavern scenes are a little more sordid, a bit more wordy, and a shade less gay.

The scenes with Justice Shallow, however, reveal the comic spirit at its best. Shakespeare's audience undoubtedly found Part 2 as funny as they had been led to expect.

The historical portions of the play follow hard on the events that had taken place in Part 1, which had ended with the victory of the King's forces over the rebels at the Battle of Shrewsbury in 1403. Part 2 begins with the renewal of the rebellion after the Battle and extends in actual time until King Henry IV's death in 1413. Shakespeare telescopes historical events that occurred over a period of more than ten years to make them appear all a part of one continuous action. This poetic license gives a unity to the play that it could not have had otherwise and does not destroy the historical implications that the author wanted to make, for his play deals with the effects of rebellion and the problems of kingship. The fact that Shakespeare found it expedient to boil several rebellions into one for dramatic effect did not alter his essential purpose.

Modern scholars have seen a parallel between the events in *Henry IV* and the Rising of the North against Queen Elizabeth in 1569, and it is likely that the similarity was not lost upon Shakespeare's audience. Certainly the lesson of the heinousness of rebellion was made explicit in the play, and even though sentimental nineteenth-century readers of Shakespeare worried about the trickery which Prince John used to capture the rebel leaders, no Elizabethan would have felt that they received less than justice. The official homilies that Queen Elizabeth caused to be printed and used in the churches had one sermon in six parts on the iniquity

of rebelliousness and the condign punishment certain
to fall upon rebels and traitors.

The old King's uneasy conscience over the way he
himself had won the crown, revealed in Part 1 when he
talks of the Crusade that he had hoped to lead, is given
greater emphasis in Part 2. The sin of regicide lay
heavy upon him, for he had connived at the murder
of Richard II when the latter was his prisoner, and
every Elizabethan understood that such a sin required
expiation. Henry believed that the rebellions that had
plagued his reign, as well as Prince Hal's erring ways,
were part of the retribution meted out to him for his
own impiousness in laying hands on the Lord's anointed
king. As he lies dying, happy at last in the knowledge
that Prince Hal bids fair to mend his ways and become
a proper king, Henry confesses his devious methods and
offers the hope that his death will atone for his iniquity
and remove from his son the threat of evil consequences:

> God knows, my son,
> By what bypaths and indirect crooked ways
> I met this crown, and I myself know well
> How troublesome it sat upon my head.
> To thee it shall descend with better quiet,
> Better opinion, better confirmation,
> For all the soil of the achievement goes
> With me into the earth.

One of Shakespeare's purposes in Part 2 is to show
the regeneration of Prince Hal and to lay the foundation
for the characterization of the hero-king in *Henry V*.
The reconciliation with the King (IV. v.), the Prince's

scene with the Chief Justice (V. ii.), and his rejection
of Falstaff (V. v.) are all part of the design to glorify
the heir-apparent and reveal him as the embodiment of
those qualities which the Elizabethans wished to see
in a sovereign. No contemporary of Shakespeare's would
have dreamed that the Prince, once the responsibility
of sovereignty had fallen on his shoulders, could do
less than cast aside the companions with whom he had
sown his wild oats in the greener times of his youth.
The fact that later critics have wasted so much ink
puzzling over "Falstaff's rejection" and the "priggish-
ness" of the Prince merely serves to show the necessity
of understanding the attitudes of Shakespeare's own age
in these matters. For the Prince to have continued to
hobnob on terms of equality with the denizens of the
Boar's Head would have violated Elizabethan notions
of the dignity inherent in an anointed king, for the
Elizabethans were convinced of the divinity enveloping
the sovereign, and it took the perversity of two later
generations of Stuart kings to wean them grudgingly
from the doctrine of divine right.

No one in Shakespeare's audience would have thought
that Prince Hal was unduly harsh in his speech in the
street to Falstaff:

> I know thee not, old man. Fall to thy prayers.
> How ill white hairs become a fool and jester!
> I have long dreamed of such a kind of man,
> So surfeit-swelled, so old, and so profane;
> But, being awaked, I do despise my dream.
>
> ....
>
> Presume not that I am the thing I was,

For God doth know, so shall the world perceive,
That I have turned away my former self.

This was merely dramatic proof of the reformation of
the young King, who, to the Elizabethans, demonstrated
his justice by promising to Falstaff and the rest of the
reprobates some royal bounty.

For competence of life I will allow you,
That lack of means enforce you not to evils;
And, as we hear you do reform yourselves,
We will, according to your strengths and qualities,
Give you advancement.

This was the kind of generosity expected of a virtuous
King, and Falstaff and his companions could not ask
for more. The modern reader's difficulty in accepting
this lies in the sympathy which the amiable old rogue
has aroused and the pleasure that we too have had in
his company. By Elizabethan standards, however, the
young King had shown his old cronies both justice and
compassion. The office of kingship carried with it a
dignity and a reserve which the King had to maintain
but which Prince Hal before his accession could tem-
porarily forget.

Shakespeare's concern to illustrate the qualities of the
just ruler in King Henry V is evident in the scene in
which Henry meets the Chief Justice who had once
reproved him and committed him to the Court of King's
Bench for interfering with a trial and striking him as he
presided. When the scene opens, none of the courtiers
is too sanguine about the behavior of the new King, and

even his brothers are gloomy. Most sorrowful of all is
the Chief Justice, who foresees his own downfall and,
worst indignity to contemplate, having to "speak Sir
John Falstaff fair." But Henry gives full assurance to
all, and Shakespeare provides a characteristically English
tribute to law and justice in the Chief Justice's
forthright statement and the King's reply:

> So shall I live to speak my father's words:
> "Happy am I, that have a man so bold
> That dares do justice on my proper son,
> And not less happy, having such a son
> That would deliver up his greatness so
> Into the hands of justice." You did commit me.
> For which, I do commit into your hand
> The unstained sword that you have used to bear,
> With this remembrance, that you use the same
> With the like bold, just, and impartial spirit
> As you have done 'gainst me.

Latent in the consciousness of Englishmen in 1598 was
the thought of the succession to the great Queen who
had now reigned forty years and in the course of nature
would soon pass to her reward. For this reason Shakespeare's
audience was interested in discussions of the
office of the sovereign and the qualities that made
the ideal king. Though the question of the succession
was not a theme permitted for public discussion, Englishmen
could hope that whatever heir succeeded to the
throne would react as Prince Hal had and measure up
to his responsibilities. As Miss Lily Bess Campbell has
clearly demonstrated, Shakespeare's two plays on Henry

IV are not mere patchworks of history interspersed with comedy, but are serious treatments of the problems of rebellion and kingship with particular interest for audiences of the author's own time.

STAGE HISTORY OF THE PLAY

The Quarto version of *The Second Part of Henry the Fourth*, published in 1600, described it as "sundry times publicly acted by the right honorable the Lord Chamberlain his servants." Although the records of contemporary performances are lost, both parts were evidently acted at both the Globe and the Blackfriars and at Court. Tradition makes Falstaff a character who delighted Queen Elizabeth so much that she demanded to see him in love and hence induced Shakespeare to write *The Merry Wives of Windsor*.

The Folger Library possesses a manuscript adaptation of the two parts of *Henry IV* into a single acting version, with alterations in the hand of Sir Edward Dering of Surrenden in Kent, who died in 1644. It appears that this version was intended for a private performance. Although Part 2 has not enjoyed the same popularity as the first part, it has been fairly regularly performed through the centuries since it was first acted. Thomas Betterton is said to have revived it about 1703 and a version attributed to Betterton was produced in 1720. Both parts enjoyed a considerable vogue in the early eighteenth century. James Quin achieved a great reputation for his interpretation of the part of Falstaff. David Garrick produced both parts and he himself played the part of the old King in Part 2 in a revival in 1758.

At intervals during the nineteenth century, Part 2 was performed with some success. Justice Shallow was a character part that brought out the comic possibilities in several popular actors, notably Samuel Phelps, and Falstaff remained of course a favored part for the best comedians. From time to time in the twentieth century the professional theatre has seen the performance of both parts of *Henry IV*. Because Part 2 depends for its success upon the build-up in Part 1, it cannot easily be made to stand alone (as Part 1 can) and hence it is less often staged. The most recent production at the Phoenix Theatre in New York in 1960 achieved a qualified success.

SOURCES

As in Part 1, the principal historical source for Part 2 is Raphael Holinshed's *The Chronicles of England* (2nd edition, 1587). Some suggestions appear to have been taken from John Stow's *Annals of England* (1592) and Samuel Daniel's poem, *The Civil Wars* (1595). The story of the Chief Justice's committal of the Prince to the Court of King's Bench is found in Sir Thomas Elyot's *The Book Named the Governor* (1531) and repeated in Stow. Some of the episodes, including the rejection of Falstaff, parallel those found in the old play *The Famous Victories of Henry the Fifth*, first acted sometime before 1588 and printed in 1598. Essentially, however, the source is Holinshed, who in turn utilized the earlier chronicle of Edward Hall, *The Union of the Two Noble and Illustrate Families, of Lancaster and York* (1548).

TEXT

The text of this edition, like that of most modern editions, is based on the Quarto of 1600, the only printed version which appeared before the appearance of the Folio of 1623, though a second issue of the Quarto is known, apparently necessitated by the omission from the first printing of the first scene of Act III. Otherwise the second issue differs from the first only in variations in spelling and a few included words that make little difference to the meaning.

Copy for the Quarto appears to have been a playhouse promptbook. A number of variations between the Quarto and the Folio versions occur. The Quarto omits a total of 168 lines of text found in the Folio and the Folio omits about 40 lines of the Quarto text. Some variations also occur in the stage directions. The Folio shows the usual evidences of toning down oaths and profane passages. The Folio, in Sir Edmund Chambers' opinion, "follows a theatrical manuscript. This may, indeed, have been the same manuscript which was used for Q, but if so, it had undergone subsequent overhauling by the bookkeeper." The present text has supplemented the Quarto text with the omitted passages contained in the Folio and adopts a few Folio readings that seem better than the corresponding ones in the Quarto.

THE AUTHOR

As early as 1598 Shakespeare was so well known as a literary and dramatic craftsman that Francis Meres, in his *Palladis Tamia: Wits Treasury,* referred in flattering terms to him as "mellifluous and honey-tongued Shakespeare," famous for his *Venus and Adonis,* his *Lucrece,* and "his sugared sonnets," which were circulating "among his private friends." Meres observes further that "as Plautus and Seneca are accounted the best for comedy and tragedy among the Latins, so Shakespeare among the English is the most excellent in both kinds for the stage," and he mentions a dozen plays that had made a name for Shakespeare. He concludes with the remark "that the Muses would speak with Shakespeare's fine filed phrase if they would speak English."

To those acquainted with the history of the Elizabethan and Jacobean periods, it is incredible that anyone should be so naïve or ignorant as to doubt the reality of Shakespeare as the author of the plays that bear his name. Yet so much nonsense has been written about other "candidates" for the plays that it is well to remind readers that no credible evidence that would stand up in a court of law has ever been adduced to prove either that Shakespeare did not write his plays or that anyone else wrote them. All the theories offered for the authorship of Francis Bacon, the Earl of Derby, the Earl of Oxford, the Earl of Hertford, Christopher Marlowe, and a score of other candidates are mere conjectures spun from the active imaginations of persons who confuse hypothesis and conjecture with evidence.

As Meres' statement of 1598 indicates, Shakespeare was already a popular playwright whose name carried weight at the box office. The obvious reputation of Shakespeare as early as 1598 makes the effort to prove him a myth one of the most absurd in the history of human perversity.

The anti-Shakespeareans talk darkly about a plot of vested interests to maintain the authorship of Shakespeare. Nobody has any vested interest in Shakespeare, but every scholar is interested in the truth and in the quality of evidence advanced by special pleaders who set forth hypotheses in place of facts.

The anti-Shakespeareans base their arguments upon a few simple premises, all of them false. These false premises are that Shakespeare was an unlettered yokel without any schooling, that nothing is known about Shakespeare, and that only a noble lord or the equivalent in background could have written the plays. The facts are that more is known about Shakespeare than about most dramatists of his day, that he had a very good education, acquired in the Stratford Grammar School, that the plays show no evidence of profound book learning, and that the knowledge of kings and courts evident in the plays is no greater than any intelligent young man could have picked up at second hand. Most anti-Shakespeareans are naïve and betray an obvious snobbery. The author of their favorite plays, they imply, must have had a college diploma framed and hung on his study wall like the one in their dentist's office, and obviously so great a writer must have had a title or some equally significant evidence of exalted social background. They forget that genius has a way of cropping up in unexpected places and that none of the great creative writers of the world got his inspiration in a college or university course.

William Shakespeare was the son of John Shakespeare

of Stratford-upon-Avon, a substantial citizen of that small but busy market town in the center of the rich agricultural county of Warwick. John Shakespeare kept a shop, what we would call a general store; he dealt in wool and other produce and gradually acquired property. As a youth, John Shakespeare had learned the trade of glover and leather worker. There is no contemporary evidence that the elder Shakespeare was a butcher, though the anti-Shakespeareans like to talk about the ignorant "butcher's boy of Stratford." Their only evidence is a statement by gossipy John Aubrey, more than a century after William Shakespeare's birth, that young William followed his father's trade, and when he killed a calf, "he would do it in a high style and make a speech." We would like to believe the story true, but Aubrey is not a very credible witness.

John Shakespeare probably continued to operate a farm at Snitterfield that his father had leased. He married Mary Arden, daughter of his father's landlord, a man of some property. The third of their eight children was William, baptized on April 26, 1564, and probably born three days before. At least, it is conventional to celebrate April 23 as his birthday.

The Stratford records give considerable information about John Shakespeare. We know that he held several municipal offices including those of alderman and mayor. In 1580 he was in some sort of legal difficulty and was fined for neglecting a summons of the Court of Queen's Bench requiring him to appear at Westminster and be bound over to keep the peace.

As a citizen and alderman of Stratford, John Shakespeare was entitled to send his son to the grammar school free. Though the records are lost, there can be no reason to doubt that this is where young William received his education. As any student of the period knows, the grammar schools provided the basic education in Latin learning and literature. The Elizabethan grammar school is not to be confused with modern grammar schools. Many cultivated men of the day received all their formal education in the grammar schools. At the universities in this period a student would have received little training that would have inspired him to be a creative writer. At Stratford young Shakespeare would have acquired a familiarity with Latin and some little knowledge of Greek. He would have read Latin authors and become acquainted with the plays of Plautus and Terence. Undoubtedly, in this period of his life he received that stimulation to read and explore for himself the world of ancient and modern history which he later utilized in his plays. The youngster who does not acquire this type of intellectual curiosity *before* college days rarely develops as a result of a college course the kind of mind Shakespeare demonstrated. His learning in books was anything but profound, but he clearly had the probing curiosity that sent him in search of information, and he had a keenness in the observation of nature and of humankind that finds reflection in his poetry.

There is little documentation for Shakespeare's boyhood. There is little reason why there should be. Nobody knew that he was going to be a dramatist about whom any scrap of information would be prized in the centuries to come. He was merely an active and vigorous youth of Stratford, perhaps assisting his father in his business, and no Boswell bothered to write down facts about him. The most important record that we have is a marriage license issued by the Bishop of Worcester on November 28, 1582, to permit William Shakespeare to marry Anne Hathaway, seven or eight years his senior; furthermore, the Bishop permitted the marriage after reading the banns only once instead of three times, evidence of the desire for haste. The need was explained on May 26, 1583, when the christening of Susanna, daughter of William and Anne Shakespeare, was recorded at Stratford. Two years later, on February 2, 1585, the records show the birth of twins to the Shakespeares, a boy and a girl who were christened Hamnet and Judith.

What William Shakespeare was doing in Stratford during the early years of his married life, or when he went to London, we do not know. It has been conjectured that he tried his hand at schoolteaching, but that is a mere guess. There is a legend that he left Stratford to escape a charge of poaching in the park of Sir Thomas Lucy of Charlecote, but there is no proof of this. There is also a legend that when first he came to London, he earned his living by holding horses outside a playhouse and presently was given employment inside, but there is nothing better than eighteenth-century hearsay for this. How Shakespeare broke into the London theatres as a dramatist and actor we do not know. But lack of information is not surprising, for Elizabethans did not write their autobiographies, and we know even less about the lives of many writers and some men of affairs than we know about Shakespeare. By 1592 he was so well established and popular that he incurred the envy of the dramatist and pamphleteer Robert Greene, who referred to him as an "upstart crow . . . in his own conceit the only Shake-scene in a country." From this time onward, contemporary allusions and references in legal documents enable the scholar to chart Shakespeare's career with greater accuracy than is possible with most other Elizabethan dramatists.

By 1594 Shakespeare was a member of the company of actors known as the Lord Chamberlain's Men. After the accession of James I, in 1603, the company would have the sovereign for their patron and would be known as the King's Men. During the period of its greatest prosperity, this company would have as its principal theatres the Globe and the Blackfriars. Shakespeare was both an actor and a shareholder in the company. Tradition has assigned him such acting roles as Adam in *As You Like It* and the Ghost in *Hamlet,* a modest place on the stage that suggests that he may have had other duties in the management of the company. Such conclusions, however, are based on surmise.

What we do know is that his plays were popular and that he was highly successful in his vocation. His first play may have been *The Comedy of Errors,* acted perhaps in 1591. Certainly this was one of his earliest plays. The three parts of *Henry VI* were acted sometime between 1590 and 1592. Critics are not in agreement about precisely how much Shakespeare wrote of these three plays. *Richard III* probably dates from 1593. With this play Shakespeare captured the imagination of Elizabethan audiences, then enormously interested in historical plays. With *Richard III* Shakespeare also gave an interpretation pleasing to the Tudors of the rise to power of the grandfather of Queen Elizabeth. From this time onward, Shakespeare's plays followed on the stage in rapid succession: *Titus Andronicus, The Taming of the Shrew, The Two Gentlemen of Verona, Love's Labour's Lost, Romeo and Juliet, Richard II, A Midsummer Night's Dream, King John, The Merchant of Venice, Henry IV (Parts 1 and 2), Much Ado About Nothing, Henry V, Julius Cæsar, As You Like It, Twelfth Night, Hamlet, The Merry Wives of Windsor, All's Well That Ends Well, Measure for Measure, Othello, King Lear,* and nine others that followed before Shakespeare retired completely, about 1613.

In the course of his career in London, he made enough money to enable him to retire to Stratford with a competence. His purchase on May 4, 1597, of New Place, then the second-largest dwelling in Stratford, a "pretty house of brick and timber," with a handsome garden, indicates his increasing prosperity. There his wife and children lived while he busied himself in the London theatres. The summer before he acquired New Place, his life was darkened by the death of his only son, Hamnet, a child of eleven. In May, 1602, Shakespeare purchased one hundred and seven acres of fertile farmland near Stratford and a few months later bought a cottage and garden across the alley from New Place. About 1611, he seems to have returned permanently to Stratford, for the next year a legal document refers to him as "William Shakespeare of Stratford-upon-Avon . . . gentleman." To achieve the desired appellation of gentleman, William Shakespeare had seen to it that the College of Heralds in 1596 granted his father a coat of arms. In one step he thus became a second-generation gentleman.

Shakespeare's daughter Susanna made a good match in 1607 with Dr. John Hall, a prominent and prosperous Stratford physician. His second daughter, Judith, did not marry until she was thirty-two years old, and then, under somewhat scandalous circumstances, she married Thomas Quiney, a Stratford vintner. On March 25, 1616, Shakespeare made his will, bequeathing his landed property to Susanna, £300 to Judith, certain sums to other relatives, and his second-best bed to his wife, Anne. Much has been made of the second-best bed, but the legacy probably indicates only that Anne liked that particular bed. Shakespeare, following the practice of the time, may have already arranged with Susanna for his wife's care. Finally, on April 23, 1616, the anniversary of his birth, William Shakespeare died, and he was buried on April 25 within the chancel of Trinity Church, as befitted an honored citizen. On August 6, 1623, a few months before the publication of the collected edition of Shakespeare's plays, Anne Shakespeare joined her husband in death.

THE PUBLICATION OF HIS PLAYS

During his lifetime Shakespeare made no effort to publish any of his plays, though eighteen appeared in print in single-play editions known as quartos. Some of these are corrupt versions known as "bad quartos." No quarto, so far as is known, had the author's approval. Plays were not considered "literature" any more than most radio and television scripts today are considered literature. Dramatists sold their plays outright to the theatrical companies and it was usually considered in the company's interest to keep plays from getting into print. To achieve a reputation as a man of letters, Shakespeare wrote his *Sonnets* and his narrative poems, *Venus and Adonis* and *The Rape of Lucrece*, but he probably never dreamed that his plays would establish his reputation as a literary genius. Only Ben Jonson, a man known for his colossal conceit, had the crust to call his plays *Works*, as he did when he published an edition in 1616. But men laughed at Ben Jonson.

After Shakespeare's death, two of his old colleagues in the King's Men, John Heminges and Henry Condell, decided that it would be a good thing to print, in more accurate versions than were then available, the plays already published and eighteen additional plays not previously published in quarto. In 1623 appeared *Mr. William Shakespeares Comedies, Histories, & Tragedies. Published according to the True Originall Copies. London. Printed by Isaac Iaggard and Ed. Blount.* This was the famous First Folio, a work that had the authority of Shakespeare's associates. The only play commonly attributed to Shakespeare that was omitted in the First Folio was *Pericles*. In their preface, "To the great Variety of Readers," Heminges and Condell state that whereas "you were abused with diverse stolen and surreptitious copies, maimed and deformed by the frauds and stealths of injurious impostors that exposed them, even those are now offered to your view cured and perfect of their limbs; and all the rest, absolute in their numbers, as he conceived them." What they used for printer's copy is one of the vexed problems of scholarship, and skilled bibliographers have devoted years of study to the question of the relation of the "copy" for the First Folio to Shakespeare's manuscripts. In some cases it is clear that the editors corrected printed quarto versions of the plays, probably by comparison with playhouse scripts. Whether these scripts were in Shakespeare's autograph is anybody's guess. No manuscript of any play in Shakespeare's handwriting has survived. Indeed, very few play manuscripts from this period by any author are extant. The Tudor and Stuart periods had not yet learned to prize autographs and authors' original manuscripts.

Since the First Folio contains eighteen plays not previously printed, it is the only source for these. For the other eighteen, which had appeared in quarto versions, the First Folio also has the authority of an edition prepared and overseen by Shakespeare's colleagues and professional associates. But since editorial standards in 1623 were far from strict, and Heminges and Condell were actors rather than editors by profession, the texts are sometimes careless. The printing and proofreading of the First Folio also left much to be desired, and some garbled passages have to be corrected and emended. The "good quarto" texts have to be taken into account in preparing a modern edition.

Because of the great popularity of Shakespeare through the centuries, the First Folio has become a prized book, but it is not a very rare one, for it is estimated that 238 copies are extant. The Folger Shakespeare Library in Washington, D.C., has seventy-nine copies of the First Folio, collected by the founder, Henry Clay Folger, who believed that a collation of as many texts as possible would reveal significant facts about the text of Shakespeare's plays. Dr. Charlton Hinman, using an ingenious machine of his own invention for mechanical collating, has made discoveries that throw light on Shakespeare's text and on printing practices of the day.

The probability is that the First Folio of 1623 had an edition of between 1,000 and 1,250 copies. It is believed that it sold for £1, which made it an expensive book, for £1 in 1623 was equivalent to something between $40 and $50 in modern purchasing power.

During the seventeenth century, Shakespeare was sufficiently popular to warrant three later editions in folio size, the Second Folio of 1632, the Third Folio of 1663–1664, and the Fourth Folio of 1685. The Third Folio added six other plays ascribed to Shakespeare, but these are apocryphal.

THE SHAKESPEAREAN THEATRE

The theatres in which Shakespeare's plays were performed were vastly different from those we know today. The stage was a platform that jutted out into the area now occupied by the first rows of seats on the main floor, what is called the "orchestra" in America and the "pit" in England. This platform had no curtain to come down at the ends of acts and scenes. And although simple stage properties were available, the Elizabethan theatre lacked both the machinery and the elaborate movable scenery of the modern theatre. In the rear of the platform stage was a curtained area that could be used as an inner room, a tomb, or any such scene that might be required. A balcony above this inner room, and perhaps balconies on the sides of the stage, could represent the upper deck of a ship, the entry to Juliet's room, or a prison window. A trap door in the stage provided an entrance for ghosts and devils from the nether regions, and a similar trap in the canopied structure over the stage, known as the "heavens," made it possible to let down angels on a rope. These primitive stage arrangements help to account for many elements in Elizabethan plays. For example, since there was no curtain, the dramatist frequently felt the necessity of writing into his play action to clear the stage at the ends of acts and scenes. The funeral march at the end of *Hamlet* is not there merely for atmosphere; Shakespeare had to get the corpses off the stage. The lack of scenery also freed the dramatist from undue concern about the exact location of his sets, and the physical relation of his various settings to each other did not have to be worked out with the same precision as in the modern theatre.

Before London had buildings designed exclusively for theatrical entertainment, plays were given in inns and taverns. The characteristic inn of the period had an inner courtyard with rooms opening onto balconies overlooking the yard. Players could set up their temporary stages at one end of the yard and audiences could find seats on the balconies out of the weather. The poorer sort could stand or sit on the cobblestones in the yard, which was open to the sky. The first theatres followed this construction, and throughout the Elizabethan period the large public theatres had a yard in front of the stage open to the weather, with two or three tiers of covered balconies extending around the theatre. This physical structure again influenced the

writing of plays. Because a dramatist wanted the actors
to be heard, he frequently wrote into his play orations
that could be delivered with declamatory effect. He also
provided spectacle, buffoonery, and broad jests to keep
the riotous groundlings in the yard entertained and
quiet.

In another respect the Elizabethan theatre differed
greatly from ours. It had no actresses. All women's roles
were taken by boys, sometimes recruited from the boys'
choirs of the London churches. Some of these youths
acted their roles with great skill and the Elizabethans
did not seem to be aware of any incongruity. The first
actresses on the professional English stage appeared
after the Restoration of Charles II, in 1660, when exiled
Englishmen brought back from France practices of the
French stage.

London in the Elizabethan period, as now, was the
center of theatrical interest, though wandering actors
from time to time traveled through the country per-
forming in inns, halls, and the houses of the nobility.
The first professional playhouse, called simply The
Theatre, was erected by James Burbage, father of
Shakespeare's colleague Richard Burbage, in 1576 on
lands of the old Holywell Priory adjacent to Finsbury
Fields, a playground and park area just north of the
city walls. It had the advantage of being outside the
city's jurisdiction and yet was near enough to be easily
accessible. Soon after The Theatre was opened, another
playhouse called The Curtain was erected in the same
neighborhood. Both of these playhouses had open
courtyards and were probably polygonal in shape.

About the time The Curtain opened, Richard Farrant,

Master of the Children of the Chapel Royal at Windsor and of St. Paul's, conceived the idea of opening a "private" theatre in the old monastery buildings of the Blackfriars, not far from St. Paul's Cathedral in the heart of the city. This theatre was ostensibly to train the choirboys in plays for presentation at Court, but Farrant managed to present plays to paying audiences and achieved considerable success until aristocratic neighbors complained and had the theatre closed. This first Blackfriars Theatre was significant, however, because it popularized the boy actors in a professional way and it paved the way for a second theatre in the Blackfriars, which Shakespeare's company took over more than thirty years later. By the last years of the sixteenth century, London had at least six professional theatres and still others were erected during the reign of James I.

The Globe Theatre, the playhouse that most people connect with Shakespeare, was erected early in 1599 on the Bankside, the area across the Thames from the city. Its construction had a dramatic beginning, for on the night of December 28, 1598, James Burbage's sons, Cuthbert and Richard, gathered together a crew who tore down the old theatre in Holywell and carted the timbers across the river to a site that they had chosen for a new playhouse. The reason for this clandestine operation was a row with the landowner over the lease to the Holywell property. The site chosen for the Globe was another playground outside of the city's jurisdiction, a region of somewhat unsavory character. Not far away was the Bear Garden, an amphitheatre devoted to the baiting of bears and bulls. This was also the region occupied by many houses of ill fame licensed by the Bishop of Winchester and the source of substantial revenue to him. But it was easily accessible either from London Bridge or by means of the cheap boats operated by the London watermen, and it had the great advantage of being beyond the authority of the Puritanical aldermen of London, who frowned on plays because they lured apprentices from work, filled their heads with improper ideas, and generally exerted a bad influence. The aldermen also complained that the crowds drawn together in the theatre helped to spread the plague.

The Globe was the handsomest theatre up to its time. It was a large building, apparently octagonal in shape and open like its predecessors to the sky in the center, but capable of seating a large audience in its covered balconies. To erect and operate the Globe, the Burbages organized a syndicate composed of the leading members of the dramatic company, of which Shakespeare was a member. Since it was open to the weather and depended on natural light, plays had to be given in the afternoon. This caused no hardship in the long afternoons of an English summer, but in the winter the weather was a great handicap and discouraged all except the hardiest. For that reason, in 1608 Shakespeare's company was glad to take over the lease of the second Blackfriars Theatre, a substantial, roomy hall reconstructed within the framework of the old monastery building. This theatre was protected from the weather and its stage was artificially lighted by chandeliers of candles. This became the winter playhouse for Shakespeare's company and at once proved so popular that the congestion of traffic created an embarrassing problem. Stringent regulations had to be made for the movement of coaches in the vicinity. Shakespeare's company continued to use the Globe during the summer months. In 1613 a squib fired from a cannon during a performance of _Henry VIII_ fell on the thatched roof and the Globe burned to the ground. The next year it was rebuilt.

London had other famous theatres. The Rose, just west of the Globe, was built by Philip Henslowe, a semiliterate denizen of the Bankside, who became one of the most important theatrical owners and producers of the Tudor and Stuart periods. What is more important for historians, he kept a detailed account book, which provides much of our information about theatrical history in his time. Another famous theatre on the Bankside was the Swan, which a Dutch priest, Johannes de Witt, visited in 1596. The crude drawing of the stage which he made was copied by his friend Arend van Buchell; it is one of the important pieces of contemporary evidence for theatrical construction. Among the other theatres, the Fortune, north of the city, on Golding Lane, and the Red Bull, even farther away from the city, off St. John's Street, were the most popular. The Red Bull, much frequented by apprentices, favored sensational and sometimes rowdy plays.

The actors who kept all of these theatres going were organized into companies under the protection of some noble patron. Traditionally actors had enjoyed a low reputation. In some of the ordinances they were classed as vagrants; in the phraseology of the time, "rogues, vagabonds, sturdy beggars, and common players" were all listed together as undesirables. To escape penalties often meted out to these characters, organized groups of actors managed to gain the protection of various personages of high degree. In the later years of Elizabeth's reign, a group flourished under the name of the Queen's Men; another group had the protection of the Lord Admiral and were known as the Lord Admiral's Men. Edward Alleyn, son-in-law of Philip Henslowe, was the leading spirit in the Lord Admiral's Men. Besides the adult companies, troupes of boy actors from time to time also enjoyed considerable popularity. Among these were the Children of Paul's and the Children of the Chapel Royal.

The company with which Shakespeare had a long association had for its first patron Henry Carey, Lord Hunsdon, the Lord Chamberlain, and hence they were known as the Lord Chamberlain's Men. After the accession of James I, they became the King's Men. This company was the great rival of the Lord Admiral's Men, managed by Henslowe and Alleyn.

All was not easy for the players in Shakespeare's time, for the aldermen of London were always eager for an excuse to close up the Blackfriars and any other theatres in their jurisdiction. The theatres outside the jurisdiction of London were not immune from interference, for they might be shut up by order of the Privy Council for meddling in politics or for various other offenses, or they might be closed in time of plague lest they spread infection. During plague times, the actors usually went on tour and played the provinces wherever they could find an audience. Particularly frightening were the plagues of 1592–1594 and 1613 when the theatres closed and the players, like many other Londoners, had to take to the country.

Though players had a low social status, they enjoyed great popularity, and one of the favorite forms of entertainment at Court was the performance of plays. To be commanded to perform at Court conferred great prestige upon a company of players, and printers frequently noted that fact when they published plays. Several of Shakespeare's plays were performed before the sovereign, and Shakespeare himself undoubtedly acted in some of these plays.

REFERENCES FOR FURTHER READING

Many readers will want suggestions for further reading about Shakespeare and his times. The literature in this field is enormous but a few references will serve as guides to further study. A simple and useful little book is Gerald Sanders, *A Shakespeare Primer* (New York, 1950). *A Companion to Shakespeare Studies* edited by Harley Granville-Barker and G. B. Harrison (Cambridge, Eng., 1934) is a valuable guide. More detailed but still not too voluminous to be confusing is Hazelton Spencer, *The Art and Life of William Shakespeare* (New York, 1940) which, like Sanders' handbook, contains a brief annotated list of useful books on various aspects of the subject. The most detailed and scholarly work providing complete factual information about Shakespeare is Sir Edmund Chambers, *William Shakespeare: A Study of Facts and Problems* (2 vols., Oxford, 1930). For detailed, factual information about the Elizabethan and seventeenth-century stages, the definitive reference works are Sir Edmund Chambers, *The Elizabethan Stage* (4 vols., Oxford, 1923) and Gerald E. Bentley, *The Jacobean and Caroline Stage* (5 vols., Oxford, 1941–1956). Alfred Harbage, *Shakespeare's Audience* (New York, 1941) and Martin Holmes, *Shakespeare's Public* (London, 1960) throw light on the nature and tastes of the customers for whom Elizabethan dramatists wrote.

Although specialists disagree about details of stage construction, the reader will find essential information in John C. Adams, *The Globe Playhouse: Its Design and Equipment* (Barnes & Noble, 1961). A model of the Globe playhouse by Dr. Adams is on permanent exhibition in the Folger Shakespeare Library in Washington, D.C. An excellent description of the architecture of the Globe is Irwin Smith, *Shakespeare's Globe Playhouse: A Modern Reconstruction in Text and Scale Drawings Based upon the Reconstruction of the Globe by John Cranford Adams* (New York, 1956). Another recent study of the physical characteristics of the Globe is C. Walter Hodges, *The Globe Restored* (London, 1953). A. M. Nagler's *Shakespeare's Stage* (New Haven, Conn., 1958) is a lucid synthesis of available information on the physical conditions in theatres of Shakespeare's age. An easily read history of the early theatres is J. Q. Adams, *Shakespearean Playhouses: A History of English Theatres from the Beginnings to the Restoration* (Boston, 1917).

The following titles on theatrical history will provide information about Shakespeare's plays in later periods: Alfred Harbage, *Theatre for Shakespeare* (Toronto, 1955); Esther Cloudman Dunn, *Shakespeare in America* (New York, 1939); George C. D. Odell, *Shakespeare from Betterton to Irving* (2 vols., London, 1921); Arthur Colby Sprague, *Shakespeare and the Actors: The Stage*

Business in His Plays (1660–1905) (Cambridge, Mass., 1944) and *Shakespearian Players and Performances* (Cambridge, Mass., 1953); Leslie Hotson, *The Commonwealth and Restoration Stage* (Cambridge, Mass., 1928); Alwin Thaler, *Shakspere to Sheridan: A Book About the Theatre of Yesterday and To-day* (Cambridge, Mass., 1922); Ernest Bradlee Watson, *Sheridan to Robertson: A Study of the 19th-Century London Stage* (Cambridge, Mass., 1926). Enid Welsford, *The Court Masque* (Cambridge, Mass., 1927) is an excellent study of the characteristics of this form of entertainment.

The question of the authenticity of Shakespeare's plays arouses perennial attention. A book that demolishes the notion of hidden cryptograms in the plays is William F. Friedman and Elizebeth S. Friedman, *The Shakespearean Ciphers Examined* (New York, 1957). A succinct account of the various absurdities advanced to suggest the authorship of a multitude of candidates other than Shakespeare will be found in R. C. Churchill, *Shakespeare and His Betters* (Bloomington, Ind., 1959) and Frank W. Wadsworth, *The Poacher from Stratford: A Partial Account of the Controversy over the Authorship of Shakespeare's Plays* (Berkeley, Calif., 1958). An essay on the curious notions in the writings of the anti-Shakespeareans is that by Louis B. Wright, "The Anti-Shakespeare Industry and the Growth of Cults," *The Virginia Quarterly Review*, XXXV (1959), 289–303.

Harley Granville-Barker, *Prefaces to Shakespeare* (5 vols., London, 1927–1948) provides stimulating critical discussion of the plays. An older classic of criticism is

Andrew C. Bradley, *Shakespearean Tragedy: Lectures on Hamlet, Othello, King Lear, Macbeth* (London, 1904), which is now available in an inexpensive reprint (New York, 1955). Thomas M. Parrott, *Shakespearean Comedy* (New York, 1949) is scholarly and readable. Shakespeare's dramatizations of English history are examined in E. M. W. Tillyard, *Shakespeare's History Plays* (London, 1948), and Lily Bess Campbell, *Shakespeare's "Histories," Mirrors of Elizabethan Policy* (San Marino, Calif., 1947) contains a more technical discussion of the same subject.

Reprints of some of the sources for Shakespeare's plays can be found in *Shakespeare's Library* (2 vols., 1850), edited by John Payne Collier, and *The Shakespeare Classics* (12 vols., 1907–1926), edited by Israel Gollancz. Geoffrey Bullough is the editor of a new series of volumes reprinting the sources, two volumes of which are in print: *Narrative and Dramatic Sources of Shakespeare. Volume 1. Early Comedies, Poems, and Romeo and Juliet* (New York, 1957); *Volume 2. The Comedies, 1597–1603* (New York, 1958). For discussion of Shakespeare's use of his sources see Kenneth Muir, *Shakespeare's Sources: Comedies and Tragedies* (London, 1957). Thomas M. Cranfill has recently edited a facsimile reprint of *Riche His Farewell to Military Profession* (1581), which contains stories probably used by Shakespeare for several of his plays.

More detailed information about *The Second Part of Henry the Fourth* may be found in several recent editions of the play: Arthur R. Humphreys (ed.), *The Second Part of the History of King Henry IV* (The Arden Shakespeare) (London, 1960); M. A. Shaaber (ed.), *A New Variorum Edition of Shakespeare: The Second Part of Henry the Fourth* (Philadelphia, 1940); and John Dover Wilson (ed.), *The Second Part of the History of Henry IV* (Cambridge, Eng., 1946).

For the historical background of *Henry IV*, James H. Wylie, *The History of England under Henry the Fourth* (4 vols., London, 1884–1898), and the same author's *The Reign of Henry the Fifth* (3 vols., Cambridge, Eng., 1914–1929) will be useful. For the way in which Shakespeare used the material in Holinshed, see *Holinshed's Chronicle as Used in Shakespeare's Plays*, edited by Allardyce Nicoll and Josephine Nicoll (Everyman's Library; New York, 1951).

The vitality of Falstaff has inspired much commentary but the interested reader may find particularly significant Maurice Morgann, *An Essay on the Dramatic Character of Sir John Falstaff* (1777; reprinted in 1912). A more recent discussion of Falstaff will be found in the entertaining *Fortunes of Falstaff* by John Dover Wilson (Cambridge, Eng., 1943).

Interesting pictures as well as new information about Shakespeare will be found in F. E. Halliday, *Shakespeare, a Pictorial Biography* (London, 1956). Allardyce Nicoll, *The Elizabethans* (Cambridge, Eng., 1957) contains a variety of illustrations.

A brief, clear, and accurate account of Tudor history is S. T. Bindoff, *The Tudors*, in the Penguin series. A readable general history is G. M. Trevelyan, *The History of England*, first published in 1926 and available in many editions. G. M. Trevelyan, *English Social History*, first published in 1942 and also available in many editions, provides fascinating information about England in all periods. Sir John Neale, *Queen Elizabeth* (London, 1934) is the best study of the great Queen. Various aspects of life in the Elizabethan period are treated in Louis B. Wright, *Middle-Class Culture in Elizabethan England* (Chapel Hill, N. C., 1935; reprinted by Cornell University Press, 1958). *Shakespeare's England: An Account of the Life and Manners of His Age*, edited by Sidney Lee and C. T. Onions (2 vols., Oxford, 1916) provides a large amount of information on many aspects of life in the Elizabethan period. Additional detail will be found in Muriel St. C. Byrne, *Elizabethan Life in Town and Country* (Barnes & Noble, 1961).

The Folger Shakespeare Library is currently publishing a series of illustrated pamphlets on various aspects of English life in the sixteenth and seventeenth centuries. The following titles are available: Dorothy E. Mason, *Music in Elizabethan England;* Craig R. Thompson, *The English Church in the Sixteenth Century;* Louis B. Wright, *Shakespeare's Theatre and the Dramatic Tradition;* Giles E. Dawson, *The Life of William Shakespeare;* Virginia A. LaMar, *English Dress in the Age of Shakespeare;* Craig R. Thompson, *The Bible in English, 1525–1611;* Craig R. Thompson, *Schools in Tudor England;* Craig R. Thompson, *Universities in Tudor England;* Lilly C. Stone, *English Sports and Recreations;* and Conyers Read, *The Government of England under Elizabeth.*

The Actors' Names

Rumor, the Presenter.

King Henry the Fourth.

Prince Henry, afterwards crowned King Henry the Fifth.

Prince John of Lancaster, }
Humphrey of Gloucester, } sons to Henry IV and
Thomas of Clarence, } brethren to Henry V.

[Earl of] Northumberland, }
[Richard Scroop,] the Archbishop of York, }
[Lord] Mowbray, }
[Lord] Hastings, } opposites against
[Thomas,] Lord Bardolph, } King Henry IV.
Travers, }
Morton, }
[Sir John] Coleville, }

[Earl of] Warwick, }
[Earl of] Westmoreland, }
[Earl of] Surrey, }
[Sir John Blunt], } of the King's party.
Gower, }
Harcourt, }
Lord Chief Justice, }

[Robert] Shallow, } both country justices.
Silence, }

Poins, }
[Sir John] Falstaff, }
Bardolph, } irregular
Pistol, } humorists.
Peto, }
Page, }

Davy, servant to Shallow.

Fang and Snare, two sergeants.

[Ralph] Mouldy, }
[Simon] Shadow, }
[Thomas] Wart, } country soldiers.
[Francis] Feeble, }
[Peter] Bullcalf, }

xl

Northumberland's Wife.
Percy's Widow.
Hostess Quickly.
Doll Tearsheet.
Epilogue [a dancer].

Drawers, Beadles, Grooms, [Porter, Messenger, Sol-
    diers, Lords, Attendants, Servants].

[SCENE: *England.*]

THE HISTORY OF
HENRY
THE FOURTH
[PART 2]

ACT I

Ind. Rumor, serving as Prologue, describes how false reports have flooded the kingdom after the Battle of Shrewsbury. Hotspur's father, who stayed away from the Battle on pretense of sickness, has been falsely comforted with news of his son's success.

|||||||||||||||||||||||||||||||||||||||

Ent. Rumor . . . tongues: Elizabethan audiences were still familiar with personified abstractions, which had been characteristic of morality plays.

3. **from the Orient to the drooping west:** i.e., following the course of the sun from the east to its setting in the west; therefore, all day long.

4. **still:** continually.

12. **Make fearful musters:** raise troops out of fear.

16. **surmises:** synonymous with **jealousies:** suspicions.

17. **of so easy and so plain a stop:** so easily played upon.

18. **blunt:** dull; stupid; **monster . . . heads:** i.e., the populace.

19. **still-discordant wavering:** continuously disagreeing and shifting opinion.

21. **anatomize:** dissect; analyze.

22. **my household:** i.e., those who know me well; my present audience.

INDUCTION

Enter *Rumor,* painted full of tongues.

Rumor. Open your ears, for which of you will stop
The vent of hearing when loud Rumor speaks?
I, from the Orient to the drooping west,
Making the wind my post horse, still unfold
The acts commenced on this ball of earth.   5
Upon my tongues continual slanders ride,
The which in every language I pronounce,
Stuffing the ears of men with false reports.
I speak of peace while covert enmity
Under the smile of safety wounds the world.   10
And who but Rumor, who but only I,
Make fearful musters and prepared defense
Whiles the big year, swol'n with some other grief,
Is thought with child by the stern tyrant war,
And no such matter? Rumor is a pipe   15
Blown by surmises, jealousies, conjectures,
And of so easy and so plain a stop
That the blunt monster with uncounted heads,
The still-discordant wavering multitude,
Can play upon it. But what need I thus   20
My well-known body to anatomize
Among my household? Why is Rumor here?
I run before King Harry's victory,

I

29. **Harry Monmouth:** a common appellation for Prince Henry, who was born at Monmouth.

34. **royal field:** battlefield where royalty fought.

37. **crafty-sick:** pretending sickness for the sake of policy; **The . . . on:** the messengers come with tiresome repetition.

∎∎∎∎∎∎∎∎∎∎∎∎∎∎∎∎∎∎∎∎∎∎∎∎∎∎∎∎∎∎∎

I. [i.] In keeping with Rumor's Induction, Lord Bardolph bears good news to Northumberland, but another messenger almost immediately reports the true story. This second report is confirmed by a third messenger and Northumberland is forced to accept his son's death and the utter defeat of their party. He is now resolved to drop his pretense of sickness, and hearing that the Archbishop of York has already raised another rebellion, he thinks of revenge.

∎∎∎∎∎∎∎∎∎∎∎∎∎∎∎∎∎∎∎∎∎∎∎

Ent. Lord Bardolph: Thomas, fifth Baron Bardolph, a historical character who was the ally of Northumberland. He is not to be confused with the comic character of the same name.

Who in a bloody field by Shrewsbury
Hath beaten down young Hotspur and his troops,   25
Quenching the flame of bold rebellion
Even with the rebels' blood. But what mean I
To speak so true at first? My office is
To noise about that Harry Monmouth fell
Under the wrath of noble Hotspur's sword,   30
And that the King before the Douglas' rage
Stooped his anointed head as low as death.
This have I rumored through the peasant towns
Between that royal field of Shrewsbury
And this worm-eaten hold of ragged stone,   35
Where Hotspur's father, old Northumberland,
Lies crafty-sick. The posts come tiring on,
And not a man of them brings other news
Than they have learned of me. From Rumor's tongues
They bring smooth comforts false, worse than true   40
     wrongs.
                                        Exit Rumor.

ACT I

Scene [I. The same.]

Enter the *Lord Bardolph* at one door.

L. Bar. Who keeps the gate here, ho?

[Enter the *Porter.*]

                                   Where is the Earl?
Port. What shall I say you are?
L. Bar.   Tell thou the Earl

5. **attend:** await.

12. **stratagem:** violent deed.

18. **an:** if.

25. **brawn:** fattened swine.

30. **How is this derived:** what is the source of this information.

Fama, or Rumor, personified.
From Vincenzo Cartari, *Imagines deorum* (1581).
(See Ent. Rumor, p. 1.)

That the Lord Bardolph doth attend him here.   5
  Port. His lordship is walked forth into the orchard.
Please it your honor, knock but at the gate,
And he himself will answer.

Enter *Northumberland.*

  L. Bar.   Here comes the Earl.
                           [*Exit Porter.*]
  North. What news, Lord Bardolph? Every minute   10
  now
Should be the father of some stratagem.
The times are wild. Contention, like a horse
Full of high feeding, madly hath broke loose
And bears down all before him.   15
  L. Bar.   Noble earl,
I bring you certain news from Shrewsbury.
  North. Good, an God will!
  L. Bar.   As good as heart can wish.
The King is almost wounded to the death;   20
And, in the fortune of my lord your son,
Prince Harry slain outright; and both the Blunts
Killed by the hand of Douglas. Young Prince John
And Westmoreland and Stafford fled the field;
And Harry Monmouth's brawn, the hulk Sir John,   25
Is prisoner to your son. O, such a day,
So fought, so followed, and so fairly won,
Came not till now to dignify the times
Since Cæsar's fortunes!
  North.   How is this derived?   30
Saw you the field? Came you from Shrewsbury?

35. **these news: news** was commonly plural in Elizabethan usage because the word derived from the Latin *res novae* (new things).

39. **overrode:** passed.

41. **haply:** perhaps.

47. **forspent:** exhausted.

55. **jade:** horse.

58. **Staying:** waiting for; **question:** conversation.

L. Bar. I spake with one, my lord, that came from
   thence,
A gentleman well bred and of good name,
That freely rendered me these news for true.   35
   North. Here comes my servant Travers, whom I
      sent
On Tuesday last to listen after news.

Enter *Travers.*

L. Bar. My lord, I overrode him on the way,
And he is furnished with no certainties   40
More than he haply may retail from me.
   North. Now, Travers, what good tidings comes
      with you?
   Tra. My lord, Sir John Umfrevile turned me back
With joyful tidings, and, being better horsed,   45
Outrode me. After him came spurring hard
A gentleman, almost forspent with speed,
That stopped by me to breathe his bloodied horse.
He asked the way to Chester, and of him
I did demand what news from Shrewsbury.   50
He told me that rebellion had bad luck
And that young Harry Percy's spur was cold.
With that, he gave his able horse the head,
And bending forward struck his armed heels
Against the panting sides of his poor jade   55
Up to the rowelhead, and starting so
He seemed in running to devour the way,
Staying no longer question.

65. **point:** lace used to fasten hose and breeches.

71. **hilding:** worthless.

73. **at a venture:** at random (not caring what he said).

74. **title leaf:** title page.

77. **a witnessed usurpation:** i.e., signs of the sea's encroachment.

86. **dead:** deadly pale.

North.   Ha! Again:
Said he young Harry Percy's spur was cold?   60
Of Hotspur Coldspur? That rebellion
Had met ill luck?
    L. Bar.   My lord, I'll tell you what:
If my young lord your son have not the day,
Upon mine honor, for a silken point   65
I'll give my barony. Never talk of it.
    North. Why should that gentleman that rode by
        Travers
Give then such instances of loss?
    L. Bar.   Who, he?   70
He was some hilding fellow that had stolen
The horse he rode on, and, upon my life,
Spoke at a venture. Look, here comes more news.

Enter *Morton.*

    North. Yea, this man's brow, like to a title leaf,
Foretells the nature of a tragic volume.   75
So looks the strand whereon the imperious flood
Hath left a witnessed usurpation.
Say, Morton, didst thou come from Shrewsbury?
    Mor. I ran from Shrewsbury, my noble lord,
Where hateful death put on his ugliest mask   80
To fright our party.
    North.   How doth my son and brother?
Thou tremblest, and the whiteness in thy cheek
Is apter than thy tongue to tell thy errand.
Even such a man, so faint, so spiritless,   85
So dull, so dead in look, so woebegone,

87. **Priam:** king of Troy.
93. **Stopping:** stuffing.
94. **stop:** i.e., end the power of hearing.
104. **divination:** intuitive prediction.
108. **spirit:** i.e., spirit of prophecy.
111. **fear:** something to fear; danger.

Drew Priam's curtain in the dead of night,
And would have told him half his Troy was burnt.
But Priam found the fire ere he his tongue,
And I my Percy's death ere thou reportst it,   90
This thou wouldst say, "Your son did thus and thus;
Your brother thus; so fought the noble Douglas"—
Stopping my greedy ear with their bold deeds.
But in the end, to stop my ear indeed,
Thou hast a sigh to blow away this praise,   95
Ending with "Brother, son, and all are dead."
  Mor. Douglas is living, and your brother, yet;
But, for my lord your son—
  North.   Why, he is dead.
See what a ready tongue suspicion hath!   100
He that but fears the thing he would not know
Hath by instinct knowledge from others' eyes
That what he feared is chanced. Yet speak, Morton.
Tell thou an earl his divination lies,
And I will take it as a sweet disgrace   105
And make thee rich for doing me such wrong.
  Mor. You are too great to be by me gainsaid.
Your spirit is too true, your fears too certain.
  North. Yet, for all this, say not that Percy's dead.
I see a strange confession in thine eye.   110
Thou shakest thy head and holdst it fear or sin
To speak a truth. If he be slain, say so.
The tongue offends not that reports his death;
And he doth sin that doth belie the dead,
Not he which says the dead is not alive.   115
Yet the first bringer of unwelcome news

117. **losing office:** unprofitable duty.

118. **sullen:** mournful.

124. **Rendering faint quittance:** defending himself feebly; **outbreathed:** breathless.

128. **few:** few words.

130. **bruited:** reported.

132. **metal:** "metal" (substance) and "mettle" (spirit).

137. **heavy:** "sorrowful" as well as "weighty."

144. **the appearance of the King:** decoys dressed to resemble the King.

145. **'Gan vail his stomach:** began to flag in courage.

Hath but a losing office, and his tongue
Sounds ever after as a sullen bell,
Remembered tolling a departing friend.
　L. Bar. I cannot think, my lord, your son is dead. 120
　Mor. I am sorry I should force you to believe
That which I would to God I had not seen.
But these mine eyes saw him in bloody state,
Rendering faint quittance, wearied and outbreathed,
To Harry Monmouth, whose swift wrath beat down 125
The never-daunted Percy to the earth,
From whence with life he never more sprung up.
In few, his death, whose spirit lent a fire
Even to the dullest peasant in his camp,
Being bruited once, took fire and heat away 130
From the best-tempered courage in his troops;
For from his metal was his party steeled,
Which once in him abated, all the rest
Turned on themselves, like dull and heavy lead.
And as the thing that's heavy in itself, 135
Upon enforcement flies with greatest speed,
So did our men, heavy in Hotspur's loss,
Lend to this weight such lightness with their fear
That arrows fled not swifter toward their aim
Than did our soldiers, aiming at their safety, 140
Fly from the field. Then was that noble Worcester
Too soon ta'en prisoner; and that furious Scot,
The bloody Douglas, whose well-laboring sword
Had three times slain the appearance of the King,
'Gan vail his stomach and did grace the shame 145
Of those that turned their backs, and in his flight,

153. **physic:** healing virtue.

160. **grief . . . grief:** physical distress . . . emotional distress.

161. **nice:** unmanly.

164. **quoif:** a protective covering for the head commonly worn by the sick.

165. **wanton:** effeminate.

166. **fleshed:** inspired with a taste for blood. Hunting dogs were **fleshed** by being fed with meat or blood of game.

168. **ragged'st:** roughest.

173. **feed contention in a lingering act:** sustain a prolonged struggle.

176. **rude:** violent.

Stumbling in fear, was took. The sum of all
Is that the King hath won, and hath sent out
A speedy power to encounter you, my lord,
Under the conduct of young Lancaster   150
And Westmoreland. This is the news at full.
  North. For this I shall have time enough to mourn.
In poison there is physic; and these news,
Having been well, that would have made me sick,
Being sick, have in some measure made me well.   155
And as the wretch whose fever-weakened joints,
Like strengthless hinges, buckle under life,
Impatient of his fit, breaks like a fire
Out of his keeper's arms, even so my limbs,
Weakened with grief, being now enraged with grief,   160
Are thrice themselves. Hence, therefore, thou nice
        crutch!
A scaly gauntlet now with joints of steel
Must glove this hand; and hence, thou sickly quoif!
Thou art a guard too wanton for the head   165
Which princes, fleshed with conquest, aim to hit.
Now bind my brows with iron, and approach
The ragged'st hour that time and spite dare bring
To frown upon the enraged Northumberland!
Let heaven kiss earth! Now let not Nature's hand   170
Keep the wild flood confined! Let order die!
And let this world no longer be a stage
To feed contention in a lingering act.
But let one spirit of the first-born Cain
Reign in all bosoms, that, each heart being set   175
On bloody courses, the rude scene may end,
And darkness be the burier of the dead!

178. **strained passion:** extravagant expression of emotion.

182. **'complices:** comrades; allies.

185-98. **You . . . be:** from the Folio; omitted from the Quarto; **cast the event:** weighed the ultimate outcome.

187. **make head:** assemble an army.

188. **dole:** dealing; exchange.

191. **advised:** aware.

198. **that being which was like to be:** i.e., the outcome which was likely.

199. **engaged to this loss:** committed to this unsuccessful cause.

201. **That if we wrought out life 'twas ten to one:** the chances were ten to one that we would not survive.

203. **respect:** consideration.

208-28. **The . . . him:** from the Folio; omitted from the Quarto; **up:** up in arms.

Tra. This strained passion doth you wrong, my
    lord.
  L. Bar. Sweet Earl, divorce not wisdom from your   180
    honor.
  Mor. The lives of all your loving 'complices
Lean on your health, the which, if you give o'er
To stormy passion, must perforce decay.
You cast the event of war, my noble lord,   185
And summed the account of chance, before you said,
"Let us make head." It was your presurmise
That, in the dole of blows, your son might drop.
You knew he walked o'er perils, on an edge,
More likely to fall in than to get o'er.   190
You were advised his flesh was capable
Of wounds and scars and that his forward spirit
Would lift him where most trade of danger ranged.
Yet did you say, "Go forth." And none of this,
Though strongly apprehended, could restrain   195
The stiff-borne action. What hath then befallen,
Or what hath this bold enterprise brought forth,
More than that being which was like to be?
  L. Bar. We all that are engaged to this loss
Knew that we ventured on such dangerous seas   200
That if we wrought out life 'twas ten to one.
And yet we ventured, for the gain proposed
Choked the respect of likely peril feared.
And since we are o'erset, venture again.
Come, we will all put forth, body and goods.   205
  Mor. 'Tis more than time. And, my most noble lord,
I hear for certain, and dare speak the truth,
The gentle Archbishop of York is up

209. **well-appointed:** well-furnished; **powers:** forces.

211. **corpse:** body.

212. **the shows of men:** creatures who only appeared to be manly.

223-24. **doth enlarge his rising with the blood/Of fair King Richard, scraped from Pomfret stones:** adds to the number of his rebels by invoking the blood of Richard II, who was murdered (supposedly at Henry IV's instigation) at Pomfret Castle.

227. **Bolingbroke:** King Henry IV.

228. **more and less:** men of all conditions.

231. **counsel every man:** let every man consider.

With well-appointed powers. He is a man
Who with a double surety binds his followers.   210
My lord your son had only but the corpse,
But shadows and the shows of men, to fight.
For that same word "rebellion" did divide
The action of their bodies from their souls,
And they did fight with queasiness, constrained,   215
As men drink potions, that their weapons only
Seemed on our side; but for their spirits and souls,
This word "rebellion," it had froze them up,
As fish are in a pond. But now the Bishop
Turns insurrection to religion.   220
Supposed sincere and holy in his thoughts,
He's followed both with body and with mind,
And doth enlarge his rising with the blood
Of fair King Richard, scraped from Pomfret stones;
Derives from heaven his quarrel and his cause;   225
Tells them he doth bestride a bleeding land,
Gasping for life under great Bolingbroke;
And more and less do flock to follow him.

 North. I knew of this before; but, to speak truth,
This present grief had wiped it from my mind.   230
Go in with me, and counsel every man
The aptest way for safety and revenge.
Get posts and letters, and make friends with speed.
Never so few, and never yet more need.

                              Exeunt.

I. [ii.] Falstaff meets his old adversary, the Lord Chief Justice, who is not pleased that Falstaff escaped without punishment for his Gad's Hill escapade. The fat rogue's wit and the fact that he has a commission from Prince Henry to join Prince John against the rebellion of the Archbishop of York are too much for the Justice. Falstaff's concern at the moment is to discover some way to secure the funds he needs for his expedition.

⁞⁞⁞⁞⁞⁞⁞⁞⁞⁞⁞⁞⁞⁞⁞⁞⁞⁞⁞⁞⁞⁞⁞⁞⁞⁞⁞⁞

Ent. **buckler:** shield.

4. **owed:** owned.

5. **mo:** more; **knew for:** was aware of.

6. **gird at:** jest upon.

7. **foolish compounded clay-man:** man of earth, compounded of folly.

8. **intends:** inclines.

14. **whoreson:** a term of good-natured abuse.

15. **mandrake:** the root of the plant *mandragora officinarum* is forked and was believed to resemble a man. Obviously, the page is very small.

16. **manned with:** attended by.

17. **agate:** a small stone used for ring settings, or a human figure carved on such a stone.

19. **juvenal:** youth.

20. **fledged:** covered with down; i.e., he is still beardless.

23. **stick:** scruple; **face-royal:** royal face, with a pun on a coin called a "royal."

24. **not a hair amiss:** not a hair is out of place (because he has none).

Scene [II. London. A street.]

*Enter Sir John Falstaff, alone, with his Page bearing
his sword and buckler.*

Fal. Sirrah, you giant, what says the doctor to my
water?

Page. He said, sir, the water itself was a good
healthy water; but, for the party that owed it, he
might have mo diseases than he knew for.   5

Fal. Men of all sorts take a pride to gird at me. The
brain of this foolish compounded clay-man is not able
to invent anything that intends to laughter more than
I invent or is invented on me. I am not only witty in
myself, but the cause that wit is in other men. I do   10
here walk before thee like a sow that hath over-
whelmed all her litter but one. If the Prince put thee
into my service for any other reason than to set me
off, why then I have no judgment. Thou whoreson
mandrake, thou art fitter to be worn in my cap than   15
to wait at my heels. I was never manned with an
agate till now. But I will inset you neither in gold nor
silver, but in vile apparel, and send you back again
to your master, for a jewel—the juvenal, the Prince
your master, whose chin is not yet fledged. I will   20
sooner have a beard grow in the palm of my hand
than he shall get one off his cheek, and yet he will
not stick to say his face is a face-royal. God may fin-
ish it when he will, 'tis not a hair amiss yet. He may

27. **writ man:** achieved manhood.

28. **grace:** right to be called "your Grace." Falstaff puns on a second meaning, "favor."

30. **slops:** breeches of full cut.

33. **band:** bond.

34. **the glutton:** Dives; see Luke 16:24.

35. **Achitophel:** traitor. Achitophel was the accomplice and co-conspirator of Absalom, II Sam. 15–17.

36-7. **yea-forsooth:** i.e., mealy-mouthed and hypocritical; **bear . . . in hand:** string along.

38. **smooth-pates:** smooth-heads (because their hair was cut short); used contemptuously to describe the petty tradesmen of London. Most men of gentle condition wore their hair long; **high shoes:** i.e., slippers called "pantofles" with high raised soles.

39-40. **is through with them in honest taking up:** has made an honest bargain with them.

43. **'a:** he.

45. **in security:** falsely confident of safety.

46-7. **he . . . it:** his wife is unfaithful and has given him the horns of a cuckold (wronged husband). **Lightness** is equivalent to unchastity for the sake of Falstaff's pun.

50. **Smithfield:** a London market, particularly noted for the sale of livestock.

52. **Paul's:** St. Paul's Cathedral. The precincts were used for various purposes, including that of hiring servants.

54. **stews:** brothels. Falstaff refers to a proverbial saying that a man should not choose a wife in Westminster, a servant in St. Paul's, or a horse in Smithfield, lest he secure a whore, a knave, or a jade.

keep it still at a face-royal, for a barber shall never   25
earn sixpence out of it; and yet he'll be crowing as if
he had writ man ever since his father was a bachelor.
He may keep his own grace, but he's almost out of
mine, I can assure him. What said Master Dombledon
about the satin for my short cloak and my slops?   30

Page. He said, sir, you should procure him better
assurance than Bardolph. He would not take his
band and yours; he liked not the security.

Fal. Let him be damned, like the glutton! Pray
God his tongue be hotter! A whoreson Achitophel! A   35
rascally yea-forsooth knave! To bear a gentleman in
hand, and then stand upon security! The whoreson
smooth-pates do now wear nothing but high shoes,
and bunches of keys at their girdles; and if a man is
through with them in honest taking up, then they   40
must stand upon security. I had as lief they would
put ratsbane in my mouth as offer to stop it with security. I looked 'a should have sent me two-and-
twenty yards of satin, as I am a true knight, and he
sends me security. Well, he may sleep in security, for   45
he hath the horn of abundance, and the lightness of
his wife shines through it. And yet cannot he see,
though he have his own lantern to light him. Where's
Bardolph?

Page. He's gone into Smithfield to buy your wor-   50
ship a horse.

Fal. I bought him in Paul's, and he'll buy me a
horse in Smithfield. An I could get me but a wife in
the stews, I were manned, horsed, and wived.

63. **charge:** responsibility.
72. **knave:** fellow.

Enter *Lord Chief Justice* and *Servant.*

Page. Sir, here comes the nobleman that committed   55
the Prince for striking him about Bardolph.

Fal. Wait close; I will not see him.

Just. What's he that goes there?

Serv. Falstaff, an't please your lordship.

Just. He that was in question for the robbery?   60

Serv. He, my lord. But he hath since done good
service at Shrewsbury, and, as I hear, is now going
with some charge to the Lord John of Lancaster.

Just. What, to York? Call him back again.

Serv. Sir John Falstaff!   65

Fal. Boy, tell him I am deaf.

Page. You must speak louder; my master is deaf.

Just. I am sure he is, to the hearing of anything
good. Go, pluck him by the elbow; I must speak with
him.   70

Serv. Sir John!

Fal. What! A young knave, and begging! Is there
not wars? Is there not employment? Doth not the
King lack subjects? Do not the rebels need soldiers?
Though it be a shame to be on any side but one, it is   75
worse shame to beg than to be on the worst side, were
it worse than the name of rebellion can tell how to
make it.

Serv. You mistake me, sir.

Fal. Why, sir, did I say you were an honest man?   80
Setting my knighthood and my soldiership aside, I
had lied in my throat if I had said so.

87-8. **that which grows to me:** that is, his knighthood, an inseparable part of himself.

90. **counter:** in the opposite direction from the quarry.

96. **by advice:** with the advice of his doctor.

A horned cuckold and his wife.
From an old ballad.
(See I. [ii.] 46. and notes.)

Serv. I pray you, sir, then set your knighthood and
your soldiership aside and give me leave to tell you
you lie in your throat if you say I am any other than   85
an honest man.

Fal. I give thee leave to tell me so! I lay aside that
which grows to me! If thou getst any leave of me,
hang me; if thou takest leave, thou wert better be
hanged. You hunt counter. Hence! Avaunt!   90

Serv. Sir, my lord would speak with you.

Just. Sir John Falstaff, a word with you.

Fal. My good lord! God give your lordship good
time of day. I am glad to see your lordship abroad. I
heard say your lordship was sick. I hope your lord-   95
ship goes abroad by advice. Your lordship, though not
clean past your youth, hath yet some smack of age in
you, some relish of the saltness of time in you; and I
most humbly beseech your lordship to have a reverent
care of your health.   100

Just. Sir John, I sent for you before your expedition to Shrewsbury.

Fal. An't please your lordship, I hear his Majesty
is returned with some discomfort from Wales.

Just. I talk not of his Majesty. You would not come   105
when I sent for you.

Fal. And I hear, moreover, his Highness is fallen
into this same whoreson apoplexy.

Just. Well, God mend him! I pray you, let me
speak with you.   110

Fal. This apoplexy, as I take it, is a kind of leth-
argy, an't please your lordship, a kind of sleeping in
the blood, a whoreson tingling.

115. **it original:** its origin; **study:** anxious thought.

117. **effects:** symptoms; **Galen:** a famous Greek medical authority of the second century A.D.

123. **by the heels:** i.e., by imprisonment.

128. **in respect of:** because of.

130. **some dram of a scruple:** a bit of doubt. A **dram** and a **scruple** are both small quantities in apothecaries' weights.

135. **land-service:** service in the militia.

Just. What tell you me of it? Be it as it is.

Fal. It hath it original from much grief, from study 115
and perturbation of the brain. I have read the cause
of his effects in Galen. It is a kind of deafness.

Just. I think you are fallen into the disease, for you
hear not what I say to you.

Fal. Very well, my lord, very well. Rather, an't 120
please you, it is the disease of not listening, the mal-
ady of not marking, that I am troubled withal.

Just. To punish you by the heels would amend the
attention of your ears, and I care not if I do become
your physician.   125

Fal. I am as poor as Job, my lord, but not so patient. Your lordship may minister the potion of imprisonment to me in respect of poverty; but how I
should be your patient to follow your prescriptions,
the wise may make some dram of a scruple, or indeed 130
a scruple itself.

Just. I sent for you, when there were matters
against you for your life, to come speak with me.

Fal. As I was then advised by my learned counsel
in the laws of this land-service, I did not come.   135

Just. Well, the truth is, Sir John, you live in great
infamy.

Fal. He that buckles himself in my belt cannot live
in less.

Just. Your means are very slender and your waste 140
is great.

Fal. I would it were otherwise. I would my means
were greater and my waist slenderer.

Just. You have misled the youthful Prince.

147. **gall:** rub; irritate.

153-54. **Wake not a sleeping wolf:** i.e., don't look for trouble.

155. **smell a fox:** be suspicious.

158. **wassail candle:** large candle for festive occasions.

159. **wax:** Falstaff makes a jest on a second meaning, "increase"; **approve:** prove.

161. **his:** its.

165. **Your ill angel is light:** that is, an ill (bad) angel (coin) is one which has been clipped of some of its gold content.

168. **go:** pass current; be accepted.

169. **costermongers:** street hucksters, from costard-mongers, the costard being a kind of apple.

169-70. **bearherd:** a trainer of bears used in bearbaiting; **Pregnancy:** i.e., a man of full wit.

171. **reckonings:** bills.

Fal. The young Prince hath misled me. I am the 145
fellow with the great belly, and he my dog.

Just. Well, I am loath to gall a new-healed wound.
Your day's service at Shrewsbury hath a little gilded
over your night's exploit on Gad's Hill. You may thank
the unquiet time for your quiet o'erposting that 150
action.

Fal. My lord?

Just. But since all is well, keep it so. Wake not a
sleeping wolf.

Fal. To wake a wolf is as bad as smell a fox. 155

Just. What! You are as a candle, the better part
burnt out.

Fal. A wassail candle, my lord, all tallow. If I did
say of wax, my growth would approve the truth.

Just. There is not a white hair in your face but 160
should have his effect of gravity.

Fal. His effect of gravy, gravy, gravy.

Just. You follow the young Prince up and down
like his ill angel.

Fal. Not so, my lord. Your ill angel is light, but I 165
hope he that looks upon me will take me without
weighing. And yet, in some respects, I grant, I cannot
go. I cannot tell. Virtue is of so little regard in these
costermongers' times that true valor is turned bearherd. Pregnancy is made a tapster, and hath his quick 170
wit wasted in giving reckonings. All the other gifts
appertinent to man, as the malice of this age shapes
them, are not worth a gooseberry. You that are old
consider not the capacities of us that are young; you
do measure the heat of our livers with the bitterness 175

176. **vaward:** vanguard; early part.

179-80. **characters:** symbols.

192. **marks:** a mark was worth two-thirds of a pound, or thirteen shillings and fourpence.

193. **have at him:** i.e., let him defend himself.

197. **sack:** sherry.

Soldiers, one with sword and buckler.
From an old ballad.

of your galls. And we that are in the vaward of our
youth, I must confess, are wags too.

Just. Do you set down your name in the scroll of
youth, that are written down old with all the characters of age? Have you not a moist eye, a dry hand, a   180
yellow cheek, a white beard, a decreasing leg, an increasing belly? Is not your voice broken, your wind
short, your chin double, your wit single, and every
part about you blasted with antiquity? And will you
yet call yourself young? Fie, fie, fie, Sir John!   185

Fal. My lord, I was born about three of the clock
in the afternoon, with a white head and something a
round belly. For my voice, I have lost it with halloing
and singing of anthems. To approve my youth further, I will not. The truth is, I am only old in judg-   190
ment and understanding; and he that will caper with
me for a thousand marks, let him lend me the money,
and have at him! For the box of the ear that the
Prince gave you, he gave it like a rude prince, and
you took it like a sensible lord. I have checked him   195
for it, and the young lion repents; marry, not in ashes
and sackcloth, but in new silk and old sack.

Just. Well, God send the Prince a better companion!

Fal. God send the companion a better Prince! I   200
cannot rid my hands of him.

Just. Well, the King hath severed you and Prince
Harry. I hear you are going with Lord John of Lancaster against the Archbishop and the Earl of Northumberland.   205

Fal. Yea, I thank your pretty sweet wit for it. But

207. **look you pray:** be sure to pray.

226. **bear crosses:** endure difficulties, and carry crusadoes (coins imprinted with crosses); **Commend me:** give my greetings.

228. **fillip:** strike; **three-man beetle:** heavy maul requiring three men to lift it.

232. **degrees:** degrees of age; **prevent:** forestall; anticipate.

look you pray, all you that kiss my lady Peace at
home, that our armies join not in a hot day, for, by
the Lord, I take but two shirts out with me, and I
mean not to sweat extraordinarily. If it be a hot day,   210
and I brandish anything but a bottle, I would I might
never spit white again. There is not a dangerous action can peep out his head but I am thrust upon it.
Well, I cannot last ever. But it was alway yet the
trick of our English nation, if they have a good thing,   215
to make it too common. If ye will needs say I am an
old man, you should give me rest. I would to God
my name were not so terrible to the enemy as it is. I
were better to be eaten to death with a rust than to
be scoured to nothing with perpetual motion.   220

Just. Well, be honest, be honest, and God bless
your expedition!

Fal. Will your lordship lend me a thousand pound
to furnish me forth?

Just. Not a penny, not a penny. You are too impa-   225
tient to bear crosses. Fare you well. Commend me to
my cousin Westmoreland.

> [*Exeunt Chief Justice and Servant.*]

Fal. If I do, fillip me with a three-man beetle. A
man can no more separate age and covetousness than
'a can part young limbs and lechery. But the gout   230
galls the one and the pox pinches the other, and so
both the degrees prevent my curses. Boy!

Page. Sir?

Fal. What money is in my purse?

Page. Seven groats and twopence.   235

Fal. I can get no remedy against this consumption

246. **halt:** limp; **color:** excuse.

248-49. **commodity:** profit.

‖‖‖‖‖‖‖‖‖‖‖‖‖‖‖‖‖‖‖‖‖‖‖‖‖‖‖‖‖‖‖‖‖‖‖‖‖

I. [iii.] The Archbishop, Mowbray, the Earl Marshal, and two supporters, the Lords Hastings and Bardolph, confer on ways and means to achieve their objectives. With the tragic example of Hotspur before them, they fear to oppose the King with insufficient power. Although they cannot be certain of Northumberland's support, they estimate that their present numbers will be adequate, since the King has to divide his resources in order to cope with the French and the Welsh as well as with themselves. They decide to publicize their cause and seek the support of the multitude.

‖‖‖‖‖‖‖‖‖‖‖‖‖‖‖‖‖‖‖‖‖‖‖‖‖‖‖‖

6. **allow the occasion:** acknowledge the justification; **arms:** taking arms against the King.

8. **in our means:** with our resources.

10. **puissance:** synonymous with **power.**

of the purse. Borrowing only lingers and lingers it
out, but the disease is incurable. Go bear this letter to
my Lord of Lancaster, this to the Prince, this to the
Earl of Westmoreland, and this to old Mistress   240
Ursula, whom I have weekly sworn to marry since I
perceived the first white hair of my chin. About it.
You know where to find me. [*Exit Page.*] A pox of this
gout! Or a gout of this pox! For the one or the other
plays the rogue with my great toe. 'Tis no matter if I   245
do halt; I have the wars for my color, and my pension
shall seem the more reasonable. A good wit will
make use of anything. I will turn diseases to commodity.

[*Exit.*]

Scene [III. York. The Archbishop's palace.]

Enter the *Archbishop, Thomas Mowbray (Earl
Marshal),* [and] the *Lords Hastings* and *Bardolph.*

  Arch. Thus have you heard our cause and known
    our means;
And, my most noble friends, I pray you all,
Speak plainly your opinions of our hopes.
And first, Lord Marshal, what say you to it?   5
  Mow. I well allow the occasion of our arms,
But gladly would be better satisfied
How in our means we should advance ourselves
To look with forehead bold and big enough
Upon the power and puissance of the King.   10

11. **Our present musters grow upon the file:** the list of men that we can muster at present grows.

12. **men of choice:** choice men.

13-4. **supplies:** reinforcements; **live largely in the hope/Of great Northumberland:** are mainly dependent upon Northumberland's support.

15. **incensed fire of injuries:** a fire inspired by injuries.

21. **marry:** by the Virgin Mary, with the force of "indeed."

25. **theme:** matter.

30. **lined:** reinforced, probably with a pun (lined his stomach).

33-4. **in . . . thoughts:** by an unreal conception of the forces at his command, which were much smaller than his smallest estimate.

37. **winking:** closing his eyes.

39. **forms of hope:** such hopes as are likely.

40-59. **Yes . . . else:** from the Folio; omitted from the Quarto. The difficult phrasing of this passage has made editors unhappy, but there is general agreement that the sense of it approximates the following: Yes, hope is harmful, as we shall find if this present undertaking of ours is similar to the expectation of a fine crop from seeing early spring buds, when their early appearance almost guarantees that they will perish from frost. In other words, hope is harmful when it is based on easy optimism instead of realistic estimates of the factors in a case.

Hast. Our present musters grow upon the file
To five-and-twenty thousand men of choice;
And our supplies live largely in the hope
Of great Northumberland, whose bosom burns
With an incensed fire of injuries.   15
    L. Bar. The question then, Lord Hastings, stand-
        eth thus:
Whether our present five-and-twenty thousand
May hold up head without Northumberland?
    Hast. With him, we may.   20
    L. Bar.   Yea, marry, there's the point.
But if without him we be thought too feeble,
My judgment is, we should not step too far
Till we had his assistance by the hand.
For in a theme so bloody-faced as this,   25
Conjecture, expectation, and surmise
Of aids incertain should not be admitted.
    Arch. 'Tis very true, Lord Bardolph, for indeed
It was young Hotspur's case at Shrewsbury.
    L. Bar. It was, my lord, who lined himself with   30
        hope,
Eating the air on promise of supply,
Flattering himself in project of a power
Much smaller than the smallest of his thoughts,
And so, with great imagination   35
Proper to madmen, led his powers to death,
And, winking, leaped into destruction.
    Hast. But, by your leave, it never yet did hurt
To lay down likelihoods and forms of hope.
    L. Bar. Yes, if this present quality of war,   40
Indeed the instant action, a cause on foot,

51. **offices:** service rooms; **at least:** i.e., at worst.

56. **Consent:** agree.

57-9. **surveyors:** architects; **know . . . opposite:** know our own condition and how able we are to undertake the task we face.

64. **cost:** costly object; object of expense.

66. **waste for:** exposed to destruction by; **churlish:** brutal; **tyranny:** violence.

69. **The utmost man of expectation:** all the men we could possibly expect.

Lives so in hope as in an early spring
We see the appearing buds, which to prove fruit,
Hope gives not so much warrant as despair
That frosts will bite them. When we mean to build,   45
We first survey the plot, then draw the model.
And when we see the figure of the house,
Then must we rate the cost of the erection,
Which if we find outweighs ability,
What do we then but draw anew the model   50
In fewer offices, or at least desist
To build at all? Much more, in this great work,
Which is almost to pluck a kingdom down
And set another up, should we survey
The plot of situation and the model,   55
Consent upon a sure foundation,
Question surveyors, know our own estate,
How able such a work to undergo,
To weigh against his opposite. Or else
We fortify in paper and in figures,   60
Using the names of men instead of men,
Like one that draws the model of a house
Beyond his power to build it, who, half through,
Gives o'er and leaves his part-created cost
A naked subject to the weeping clouds   65
And waste for churlish winter's tyranny.
  Hast. Grant that our hopes, yet likely of fair birth,
Should be stillborn, and that we now possessed
The utmost man of expectation,
I think we are a body strong enough,   70
Even as we are, to equal with the King.

76. **as the times do brawl:** in accordance with these warlike times.

77. **the French:** French forces made several forays against coastal regions of the island at this time and were making preparations for a general assault which the King had to take measures to prevent.

80. **sound:** echo.

89. **Who is it like should:** who is likely to.

93. **substituted:** delegated to act for him.

95-118. **Let . . . worst:** from the Folio; omitted from the Quarto.

101. **fond:** foolish; **many:** multitude.

102. **beat:** assail.

L. Bar. What, is the King but five-and-twenty
    thousand?

Hast. To us no more, nay, not so much, Lord Bar-
    dolph.   75

For his divisions, as the times do brawl,
Are in three heads: one power against the French,
And one against Glendower; perforce a third
Must take up us. So is the unfirm King
In three divided, and his coffers sound   -   80
With hollow poverty and emptiness.

Arch. That he should draw his several strengths
    together
And come against us in full puissance
Need not be dreaded.   85

Hast.   If he should do so,
He leaves his back unarmed, the French and Welsh
Baying him at the heels. Never fear that.

L. Bar. Who is it like should lead his forces
    hither?   90

Hast. The Duke of Lancaster and Westmoreland.
Against the Welsh, himself and Harry Monmouth.
But who is substituted 'gainst the French,
I have no certain notice.

Arch.   Let us on,   95
And publish the occasion of our arms.
The commonwealth is sick of their own choice;
Their overgreedy love hath surfeited.
An habitation giddy and unsure
Hath he that buildeth on the vulgar heart.   100
O thou fond many, with what loud applause
Didst thou beat heaven with blessing Bolingbroke,

104. **trimmed in thine own desires:** served up to you according to your taste.

109. **eat thy dead vomit:** proverbial: The dog is returned to his vomit again.

112. **on:** of.

119. **draw our numbers:** assemble our forces.

King Henry IV.

From Hubert Goltzius, *Antiquissima nobilissimaque Anglorum regum* (1586).

Before he was what thou wouldst have him be!
And being now trimmed in thine own desires,
Thou, beastly feeder, art so full of him   105
That thou provokest thyself to cast him up.
So, so, thou common dog, didst thou disgorge
Thy glutton bosom of the royal Richard;
And now thou wouldst eat thy dead vomit up,
And howlst to find it. What trust is in these times? 110
They that when Richard lived would have him die
Are now become enamored on his grave.
Thou that threwst dust upon his goodly head
When through proud London he came sighing on
After the admired heels of Bolingbroke   115
Criest now, "O earth, yield us that king again,
And take thou this!" O thoughts of men accursed!
Past and to come seems best, things present worst.
    Mow. Shall we go draw our numbers and set on?
    Hast. We are time's subjects, and time bids be 120
    gone.

                              [*Exeunt.*]

THE HISTORY OF
HENRY
THE FOURTH
[PART 2]

ACT II

II. i. Because Mistress Quickly has entered a suit against Falstaff for a large sum of money he owes her, several officers accost him and attempt his arrest. Bardolph and the Page are defending him when the Lord Chief Justice appears and restores order. Falstaff soon mollifies Quickly, who invites him to supper and promises to lend him more money.

||||||||||||||||||||||||||||||||

1. **entered the action:** started the lawsuit.
3. **yeoman:** subordinate; assistant.
4. **stand to't:** perform his duty valiantly.
16. **foin:** make a pass with his weapon.

ACT II

Scene I. [London. A street.]

Enter *Hostess* of the Tavern and an *Officer* or *Two*
[*Fang* and *Another; Snare* follows].

Host. Master Fang, have you entered the action?
Fang. It is entered.
Host. Where's your yeoman? Is't a lusty yeoman?
Will 'a stand to't?
Fang. [*To Officer*] Sirrah, where's Snare?   5
Host. O Lord, ay! Good Master Snare.
Snare. Here, here.
Fang. Snare, we must arrest Sir John Falstaff.
Host. Yea, good Master Snare, I have entered him
and all.   10
Snare. It may chance cost some of us our lives, for
he will stab.
Host. Alas the day! Take heed of him. He stabbed
me in mine own house, and that most beastly. In good
faith, 'a cares not what mischief he does, if his weap-   15
on be out. He will foin like any devil; he will spare
neither man, woman, nor child.

24

18. **close:** get close enough to lay hands on him.

22. **vice:** grasp.

23-4. **he's an infinitive thing upon my score:** i.e., the bill he owes me is incalculable. **Infinitive** is the Hostess' error for "infinite." Part of the comic effect of the Hostess' dialogue is achieved by having her misuse words in the manner of the later Mrs. Malaprop in Sheridan's *The Rivals.*

26. **Pie Corner:** John Stow's *Survey of London* (1598) has the following comment on Pie Corner: ". . . a way towards Smithfield, called Gilt Spur, or Knightriders' Street, of the knights and others riding that way into Smithfield, replenished with buildings on both sides up to Pie Corner, a place so called of such a sign, sometimes a fair inn for receipt of travelers, but now divided into tenements, and over against the said Pie Corner lieth Cock Lane, which runneth down to Holborn conduit."

27. **indited:** invited.

28. **the Lubber's Head in Lumbert Street:** the Leopard's Head in Lombard Street. The silkman's shop had a leopard's head on the sign.

29. **exion:** action.

31. **brought in to his answer:** taken to court to answer the charge.

32. **a long one:** i.e., a lot of money.

34. **fubbed off:** put off with false promises of payment.

38. **arrant:** notorious.

39. **malmsey-nose:** red-nosed from consumption of malmsey wine.

42. **Whose mare's dead:** what's wrong; proverbial.

Fang. If I can close with him, I care not for his thrust.

Host. No, nor I neither. I'll be at your elbow.   20

Fang. An I but fist him once! An 'a come but within my vice!

Host. I am undone by his going. I warrant you, he's an infinitive thing upon my score. Good Master Fang, hold him sure. Good Master Snare, let him not 'scape. 25 'A comes continuantly to Pie Corner—saving your manhoods—to buy a saddle; and he is indited to dinner to the Lubber's Head in Lumbert Street, to Master Smooth's the silkman. I pray you, since my exion is entered and my case so openly known to the world, 30 let him be brought in to his answer. A hundred mark is a long one for a poor lone woman to bear, and I have borne, and borne, and borne, and have been fubbed off, and fubbed off, and fubbed off, from this day to that day, that it is a shame to be thought on. 35 There is no honesty in such dealing, unless a woman should be made an ass and a beast, to bear every knave's wrong. Yonder he comes, and that arrant malmsey-nose knave, Bardolph, with him. Do your offices, do your offices. Master Fang and Master 40 Snare, do me, do me, do me your offices.

Enter Sir *John Falstaff* and *Bardolph,* and the
[*Page*] *Boy.*

Fal. How now! Whose mare's dead? What's the matter?

47. **quean:** strumpet; **channel:** gutter.

50. **honeysuckle:** homicidal.

52-3. **honeyseed:** homicide; **man-queller:** man-killer.

55. **rescue:** i.e., Falstaff has asked Bardolph to effect a **rescue** (in legal terms, a rescue from official custody).

57. **wo't:** wilt.

58. **hempseed:** one destined to die at the end of a hemp rope.

59. **scullion:** kitchen servant; **rampallian:** prostitute.

60. **fustilarian:** untidy fat woman; **catastrophe:** bottom.

63. **stand to:** support.

69. **worshipful:** worthy of reverence.

Fang. Sir John, I arrest you at the suit of Mistress Quickly. 45

Fal. Away, varlets! Draw, Bardolph. Cut me off the villain's head. Throw the quean in the channel.

Host. Throw me in the channel! I'll throw thee in the channel. Wilt thou? Wilt thou? Thou bastardly rogue! Murder, murder! Ah, thou honeysuckle villain! 50 Wilt thou kill God's officers and the King's? Ah, thou honeyseed rogue! Thou art a honeyseed, a man-queller, and a woman-queller.

Fal. Keep them off, Bardolph.

Fang. A rescue! A rescue! 55

Host. Good people, bring a rescue or two. Thou wo't, wo't thou? Thou wo't, wo't ta? Do, do, thou rogue! Do, thou hempseed!

Page. Away, you scullion! You rampallian! You fustilarian! I'll tickle your catastrophe. 60

Enter *Lord Chief Justice* and his *Men.*

Just. What is the matter? Keep the peace here, ho!

Host. Good my lord, be good to me. I beseech you, stand to me.

Just. How now, Sir John! What, are you brawling here? 65
Doth this become your place, your time and business?
You should have been well on your way to York.
Stand from him, fellow. Wherefore hangst upon him?

Host. O my most worshipful lord, an't please your Grace, I am a poor widow of Eastcheap, and he is ar- 70 rested at my suit.

77. **the mare:** the nightmare.

87. **parcel-gilt:** partly gilded; **Dolphin chamber:** a room by that name in her tavern.

88. **sea coal:** bituminous coal, as distinguished from charcoal, so called because it was transported by sea.

89. **Wheeson:** Whitsun. Whitsuntide is the week beginning with the seventh Sunday after Easter.

90. **liking:** comparing.

94. **gossip:** a term of affectionate familiarity meaning something like "crony."

97. **green:** recent; new.

Just. For what sum?

Host. It is more than for some, my lord; it is for all, all I have. He hath eaten me out of house and home; he hath put all my substance into that fat belly of his. 75 But I will have some of it out again, or I will ride thee o' nights like the mare.

Fal. I think I am as like to ride the mare, if I have any vantage of ground to get up.

Just. How comes this, Sir John? Fie! what man of 80 good temper would endure this tempest of exclamation? Are you not ashamed to enforce a poor widow to so rough a course to come by her own?

Fal. What is the gross sum that I owe thee?

Host. Marry, if thou wert an honest man, thyself 85 and the money too. Thou didst swear to me upon a parcel-gilt goblet, sitting in my Dolphin chamber, at the round table, by a sea coal fire, upon Wednesday in Wheeson week, when the Prince broke thy head for liking his father to a singing-man of Windsor, thou 90 didst swear to me then, as I was washing thy wound, to marry me and make me my lady thy wife. Canst thou deny it? Did not goodwife Keech, the butcher's wife, come in then and call me gossip Quickly? Coming in to borrow a mess of vinegar, telling us she had 95 a good dish of prawns, whereby thou didst desire to eat some, whereby I told thee they were ill for a green wound? And didst thou not, when she was gone down stairs, desire me to be no more so familiarity with such poor people, saying that ere long they should 100 call me madam? And didst thou not kiss me and bid

106. **in good case:** well off.

113. **level:** just.

114-15. **practiced upon:** taken advantage of.

119. **unpay:** make good.

120-21. **sterling . . . current:** genuine, in both cases, with a pun on **current.**

122. **sneap:** rebuke.

130. **in the effect of your reputation:** i.e., in a way that will not dishonor you.

me fetch thee thirty shillings? I put thee now to thy
Book oath. Deny it, if thou canst.

Fal. My lord, this is a poor mad soul, and she says
up and down the town that her eldest son is like you. 105
She hath been in good case, and the truth is, poverty
hath distracted her. But for these foolish officers, I
beseech you I may have redress against them.

Just. Sir John, Sir John, I am well acquainted with
your manner of wrenching the true cause the false 110
way. It is not a confident brow, nor the throng of
words that come with such more than impudent
sauciness from you, can thrust me from a level consideration. You have, as it appears to me, practiced
upon the easy-yielding spirit of this woman, and 115
made her serve your uses both in purse and in person.

Host. Yea, in truth, my lord.

Just. Pray thee, peace. Pay her the debt you owe
her and unpay the villainy you have done her. The
one you may do with sterling money, and the other 120
with current repentance.

Fal. My lord, I will not undergo this sneap without
reply. You call honorable boldness impudent sauciness. If a man will make curtsy and say nothing, he is
virtuous. No, my lord, my humble duty remembered, 125
I will not be your suitor. I say to you, I do desire
deliverance from these officers, being upon hasty employment in the King's affairs.

Just. You speak as having power to do wrong. But
answer in the effect of your reputation, and satisfy the 130
poor woman.

Fal. Come hither, hostess.

142. **fain:** forced.

144. **Glasses . . . is the only drinking:** though precious metals were still in use for drinking vessels, the use of glass goblets became fashionable during the last decades of the sixteenth century.

146. **waterwork:** i.e., water color. Painted hangings and wall paintings were very popular, particularly among those who could not afford tapestry. The references are to popular subjects, such as the story of the Prodigal Son.

149. **humors:** whims.

151. **draw:** withdraw.

157. **make other shift:** find the money I need some other way.

Enter a *Messenger* [*Gower*].

Just. Now, Master Gower, what news?

Gow. The King, my lord, and Harry Prince of
Wales   135
Are near at hand. The rest the paper tells.

Fal. As I am a gentleman.

Host. Faith, you said so before.

Fal. As I am a gentleman. Come, no more words of
it.   140

Host. By this heavenly ground I tread on, I must
be fain to pawn both my plate and the tapestry of my
dining chambers.

Fal. Glasses, glasses, is the only drinking. And for
thy walls, a pretty slight drollery, or the story of the 145
Prodigal, or the German hunting in waterwork, is
worth a thousand of these bed-hangings and these
fly-bitten tapestries. Let it be ten pound, if thou canst.
Come, an 'twere not for thy humors, there's not a
better wench in England. Go, wash thy face, and 150
draw the action. Come, thou must not be in this
humor with me. Dost not know me? Come, come, I
know thou wast set on to this.

Host. Pray thee, Sir John, let it be but twenty
nobles. I' faith, I am loath to pawn my plate, so God 155
save me, la!

Fal. Let it alone; I'll make other shift. You'll be a
fool still.

Host. Well, you shall have it, though I pawn my

162. **Will I live:** as surely as I hope to live.

163. **Hook on:** don't let her get away (or change her mind).

170. **Basingstoke:** a town in Hampshire.

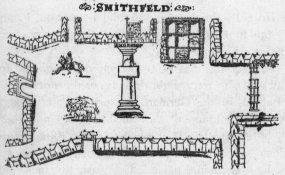

Smithfield market.
From Hugh Alley, *A Caveat for the City of London* (1598).

gown. I hope you'll come to supper. You'll pay me all   160
together?

Fal. Will I live? [*To Bardolph*] Go, with her, with
her. Hook on, hook on.

Host. Will you have Doll Tearsheet meet you at
supper?   165

Fal. No more words. Let's have her.

    Exeunt Hostess and Sergeant [*Fang, Bardolph,*
                    and others].

Just. I have heard better news.

Fal. What's the news, my lord?

Just. Where lay the King last night?

Gow. At Basingstoke, my lord.   170

Fal. I hope, my lord, all's well. What is the news,
my lord?

Just. Come all his forces back?

Gow. No. Fifteen hundred foot, five hundred horse,
Are marched up to my lord of Lancaster,   175
Against Northumberland and the Archbishop.

Fal. Comes the King back from Wales, my noble
lord?

Just. You shall have letters of me presently.
Come, go along with me, good Master Gower.   180

Fal. My lord!

Just. What's the matter?

Fal. Master Gower, shall I entreat you with me to
dinner?

Gow. I must wait upon my good lord here, I thank   185
you, good Sir John.

Just. Sir John, you loiter here too long, being you
are to take soldiers up in counties as you go.

193-94. **right fencing grace:** best fencing technique; **fair:** even.

195. **lighten:** enlighten.

░░░░░░░░░░░░░░░░░░░░░░░░░░░░░░░░░░

II. ii. Prince Hal is criticized by his friend Poins for playing the fool when his own father is seriously ill, but the Prince points out that he would only appear a hypocrite if he showed his true feelings to such companions as Poins, and he hints that he should not be judged until his career is over. Bardolph and the Page inform them that Falstaff dines that night at the Boar's Head Tavern, and the Prince suggests that he and Poins disguise themselves as waiters at the tavern and spy on Falstaff.

░░░░░░░░░░░░░░░░░░░░░░░░░░░░

3. **attached:** seized upon.

4-5. **discolors the complexion of my greatness:** causes my greatness to blush; is a shameful thing for one of my greatness.

6. **small beer:** weak beer; also, things of little consequence.

7-8. **so loosely studied as to remember so weak a composition:** so poorly versed in the behavior becoming a prince as to remember something so trivial.

9. **Belike:** probably.

10. **got:** begotten.

16. **bear:** bear in mind.

Fal. Will you sup with me, Master Gower?

Just. What foolish master taught you these man- 190
ners, Sir John?

Fal. Master Gower, if they become me not, he was
a fool that taught them me. This is the right fencing
grace, my lord—tap for tap, and so part fair.

Just. Now the Lord lighten thee! Thou art a great 195
fool.

[*Exeunt.*]

Scene II. [London. Another street.]

Enter *Prince Henry* and *Poins.*

Prince. Before God, I am exceeding weary.

Poins. Is't come to that? I had thought weariness
durst not have attached one of so high blood.

Prince. Faith, it does me, though it discolors the
complexion of my greatness to acknowledge it. Doth 5
it not show vilely in me to desire small beer?

Poins. Why, a prince should not be so loosely
studied as to remember so weak a composition.

Prince. Belike, then, my appetite was not princely
got, for, by my troth, I do now remember the poor 10
creature, small beer. But indeed these humble con-
siderations make me out of love with my greatness.
What a disgrace is it to me to remember thy name! or
to know thy face tomorrow! or to take note how many
pair of silk stockings thou hast, viz., these, and those 15
that were thy peach-colored ones! or to bear the in-

17. **superfluity:** a spare.

19-22. **for . . . holland:** i.e., Poins gives up the pleasure of tennis only when he is low in funds, as he has been for some time, because his other sensual tastes have consumed most of his money. **Low countries** equals lower (private) parts of the body. **Holland** is the name of a type of linen cloth.

22-4. **And . . . kingdom:** probably, God knows whether your bastard children shall achieve salvation.

37. **Go to:** that's enough. Usually an exclamation of impatience; **stand the push:** am ready to endure. Poins assumes that the Prince is leading up to a jest at his expense.

39. **meet:** suitable.

41. **fault:** default; lack.

46-7. **obduracy and persistency:** obstinate adherence to a wicked life; **Let the end try the man:** a proverbial idea: The end crowns all. In other words, a man should be judged by the sum of his life.

ventory of thy shirts, as, one for superfluity, and another for use! But that the tennis-court keeper knows
better than I; for it is a low ebb of linen with thee
when thou keepest not racket there, as thou hast not   20
done a great while, because the rest of thy low countries have made a shift to eat up thy holland. And
God knows whether those that bawl out the ruins of
thy linen shall inherit His kingdom. But the midwives
say the children are not in the fault, whereupon the   25
world increases, and kindreds are mightily strength-
ened.

Poins. How ill it follows, after you have labored so
hard, you should talk so idly! Tell me, how many
good young princes would do so, their fathers being   30
so sick as yours at this time is?

Prince. Shall I tell thee one thing, Poins?

Poins. Yes, faith, and let it be an excellent good
thing.

Prince. It shall serve among wits of no higher   35
breeding than thine.

Poins. Go to. I stand the push of your one thing
that you will tell.

Prince. Marry, I tell thee, it is not meet that I
should be sad, now my father is sick. Albeit I could   40
tell to thee, as to one it pleases me, for fault of a better, to call my friend, I could be sad, and sad indeed
too.

Poins. Very hardly upon such a subject.

Prince. By this hand, thou thinkest me as far in the   45
Devil's book as thou and Falstaff for obduracy and
persistency. Let the end try the man. But I tell thee,

50. **ostentation:** display.

57-8. **keeps the roadway:** follows the common course.

59. **accites:** moves; inspires.

61. **lewd:** vile; ignoble.

62. **engraffed:** attached; connected.

66-7. **a second brother:** i.e., poor, since his father's estate would go to the eldest son; **a proper fellow of my hands:** a fine man in a brawl.

my heart bleeds inwardly that my father is so sick.
And keeping such vile company as thou art hath in
reason taken from me all ostentation of sorrow.   50

Poins. The reason?

Prince. What wouldst thou think of me if I should
weep?

Poins. I would think thee a most princely hypocrite.

Prince. It would be every man's thought, and thou   55
art a blessed fellow to think as every man thinks.
Never a man's thought in the world keeps the roadway better than thine. Every man would think me an
hypocrite indeed. And what accites your most worshipful thought to think so?   60

Poins. Why, because you have been so lewd and so
much engraffed to Falstaff.

Prince. And to thee.

Poins. By this light, I am well spoke on; I can hear
it with mine own ears. The worst that they can say   65
of me is that I am a second brother and that I am a
proper fellow of my hands, and those two things I
confess I cannot help. By the mass, here comes
Bardolph.

Enter *Bardolph* and [*Page*] *Boy*.

Prince. And the boy that I gave Falstaff. 'A had   70
him from me Christian, and look if the fat villain have
not transformed him ape.

Bar. God save your Grace!

Prince. And yours, most noble Bardolph!

Poins. Come, you virtuous ass, you bashful fool,   75

76. **must you be blushing:** a gibe at Bardolph's red face.

78. **get a pottle-pot's maidenhead:** consume a two-quart measure of ale.

79-80. **through a red lattice:** many alehouses had windows with red lattices.

82. **petticoat:** i.e., scarlet petticoat, a garment prized by whores.

84. **profited:** become proficient in clever talk.

86. **Althaea's dream:** firebrand. Intentionally or not, Shakespeare has confused the stories of Althaea and Hecuba. It was Hecuba who dreamed of giving birth to a firebrand, while Althaea's firebrand was real.

94. **cankers:** cankerworms.

100. **good respect:** suitable deference (ironical).

101. **martlemas:** martlemas beef; that is, a beef fattened for killing on Martinmas Day (November 11), the traditional time for slaughtering.

106. **wen:** encysted tumor; abnormal growth.

must you be blushing? Wherefore blush you now?
What a maidenly man-at-arms are you become! Is't
such a matter to get a pottle-pot's maidenhead?

Page. 'A calls me e'en now, my lord, through a red
lattice, and I could discern no part of his face from 80
the window. At last I spied his eyes, and methought
he had made two holes in the alewife's new petticoat
and so peeped through.

Prince. Has not the boy profited?

Bar. Away, you whoreson upright rabbit, away! 85

Page. Away, you rascally Althaea's dream, away!

Prince. Instruct us, boy. What dream, boy?

Page. Marry, my lord, Althaea dreamed she was
delivered of a firebrand, and therefore I call him her
dream. 90

Prince. A crown's worth of good interpretation.
There 'tis, boy.

Poins. O that this good blossom could be kept from
cankers! Well, there is sixpence to preserve thee.

Bar. An you do not make him hanged among you, 95
the gallows shall have wrong.

Prince. And how doth thy master, Bardolph?

Bar. Well, my lord. He heard of your Grace's
coming to town. There's a letter for you.

Poins. Delivered with good respect. And how doth 100
the martlemas, your master?

Bar. In bodily health, sir.

Poins. Marry, the immortal part needs a physician,
but that moves not him. Though that be sick, it dies
not. 105

Prince. I do allow this wen to be as familiar with

114. **takes upon him not to conceive:** pretends not to understand.

115. **ready as a borrower's cap:** the allusion is to the quickness with which a would-be borrower shows deference by doffing his cap. The Quarto and Folio both read "borrowed"; "borrower's" was first suggested by Lewis Theobald.

118. **fetch it from Japhet:** trace their lineage back to Japhet, the son of Noah who was believed to have been the ancestor of all European peoples.

121. **certificate:** legal instrument.

126. **commend me:** tender my respects.

me as my dog, and he holds his place, for look you
how he writes.

Poins. [*Reads*] "John Falstaff, knight"—every man
must know that, as oft as he has occasion to name 110
himself. Even like those that are kin to the King, for
they never prick their finger but they say, "There's
some of the King's blood spilt." "How comes that?"
says he that takes upon him not to conceive. The answer is as ready as a borrower's cap, "I am the King's 115
poor cousin, sir."

Prince. Nay, they will be kin to us, or they will
fetch it from Japhet. But to the letter. [*Reads*] "Sir
John Falstaff, knight, to the son of the King, nearest
his father, Harry Prince of Wales, greeting." 120

Poins. Why, this is a certificate.

Prince. Peace! [*Reads*] "I will imitate the honorable Romans in brevity."

Poins. He sure means brevity in breath, short-
winded. 125

Prince. [*Reads*] "I commend me to thee, I commend thee, and I leave thee. Be not too familiar with
Poins, for he misuses thy favors so much that he
swears thou art to marry his sister Nell. Repent at idle
times as thou mayest, and so farewell. 130

"Thine, by yea and no, which is as much as to
say, as thou usest him, Jack Falstaff with my fa-
miliars, John with my brothers and sisters, and
Sir John with all Europe."

Poins. My lord, I'll steep this letter in sack and 135
make him eat it.

Prince. That's to make him eat twenty of his words.

147. **frank:** sty.

150. **Ephesians:** good fellows.

154. **pagan:** whore.

167. **should:** must; **road:** common passage; that is, whore.

Jupiter (Jove) and Europa.
From Ovid, *Metamorphoses* (1565).
(See II. ii. 175. and note.)

But do you use me thus, Ned? Must I marry your
sister?

Poins. God send the wench no worse fortune! But I 140
never said so.

Prince. Well, thus we play the fools with the time,
and the spirits of the wise sit in the clouds and mock
us. Is your master here in London?

Bar. Yea, my lord.   145

Prince. Where sups he? Doth the old boar feed in
the old frank?

Bar. At the old place, my lord, in Eastcheap.

Prince. What company?

Page. Ephesians, my lord, of the old church.   150

Prince. Sup any women with him?

Page. None, my lord, but old Mistress Quickly and
Mistress Doll Tearsheet.

Prince. What pagan may that be?

Page. A proper gentlewoman, sir, and a kinswoman   155
of my master's.

Prince. Even such kin as the parish heifers are to
the town bull. Shall we steal upon them, Ned, at supper?

Poins. I am your shadow, my lord; I'll follow you. 160

Prince. Sirrah, you boy, and Bardolph, no word to
your master that I am yet come to town. There's for
your silence.

Bar. I have no tongue, sir.

Page. And for mine, sir, I will govern it.   165

Prince. Fare you well; go. [*Exeunt Bardolph and
Page.*] This Doll Tearsheet should be some road.

170. **bestow himself:** perform.

173. **drawers:** i.e., drawers of ale; waiters.

174. **heavy descension:** great comedown.

175. **Jove's case:** Jove courted Europa in the likeness of a bull; **prentice:** apprentice tapster.

‖‖‖‖‖‖‖‖‖‖‖‖‖‖‖‖‖‖‖‖‖‖‖‖‖‖‖‖‖‖‖‖‖‖‖‖

II. iii. Northumberland's wife and daughter-in-law try to dissuade him from joining the rebellion against Henry IV; he is finally induced to retreat to Scotland until it is possible to estimate the strength of the Archbishop's forces against those of the King.

‖‖‖‖‖‖‖‖‖‖‖‖‖‖‖‖‖‖‖‖‖‖‖‖‖‖

2. **daughter:** daughter-in-law.

3. **Give even way unto:** allow full liberty to; **rough affairs:** military enterprise.

9. **but my going:** unless I go.

12. **endeared:** bound, possibly with an overtone of "when it should have been more dear to you" because of the effect his participation would have had on his son's fortunes.

Poins. I warrant you, as common as the way between St. Albans and London.

Prince. How might we see Falstaff bestow himself 170
tonight in his true colors, and not ourselves be seen?

Poins. Put on two leathern jerkins and aprons, and
wait upon him at his table as drawers.

Prince. From a God to a bull? A heavy descension!
It was Jove's case. From a prince to a prentice? A low 175
transformation! That shall be mine, for in everything
the purpose must weigh with the folly. Follow me,
Ned.

Exeunt.

Scene III. [Warkworth. Before the castle.]

Enter *Northumberland,* his *Wife,* and the
Wife to *Harry Percy.*

North. I pray thee, loving wife, and gentle
daughter,
Give even way unto my rough affairs.
Put not you on the visage of the times
And be like them to Percy troublesome. 5

Wife. I have given over, I will speak no more.
Do what you will, your wisdom be your guide.

North. Alas, sweet wife, my honor is at pawn,
And, but my going, nothing can redeem it.

Lady P. O yet, for God's sake, go not to these wars! 10
The time was, father, that you broke your word,
When you were more endeared to it than now,

18. **For:** as for.

22. **glass:** mirror.

24-46. **He . . . grave:** from the Folio; omitted from the Quarto; **He had no legs that practiced not his gait:** that is, everyone strove to walk as Hotspur did.

27. **tardily:** slowly.

30. **affections of delight:** inclinations to pleasure.

31. **humors of blood:** disposition.

37. **abide a field:** face a battle.

39. **defensible:** capable of defensive action.

41. **precise and nice:** synonymous; i.e., to be more punctilious about your honor.

When your own Percy, when my heart's dear Harry,
Threw many a northward look to see his father
Bring up his powers, but he did long in vain.   15
Who then persuaded you to stay at home?
There were two honors lost, yours and your son's.
For yours, the God of heaven brighten it!
For his, it stuck upon him as the sun
In the grey vault of heaven, and by his light   20
Did all the chivalry of England move
To do brave acts. He was indeed the glass
Wherein the noble youth did dress themselves.
He had no legs that practiced not his gait;
And speaking thick, which nature made his blemish,   25
Became the accents of the valiant,
For those that could speak low and tardily
Would turn their own perfection to abuse,
To seem like him. So that in speech, in gait,
In diet, in affections of delight,   30
In military rules, humors of blood,
He was the mark and glass, copy and book,
That fashioned others. And him—O wondrous him!
O miracle of men!—him did you leave,
Second to none, unseconded by you,   35
To look upon the hideous god of war
In disadvantage, to abide a field
Where nothing but the sound of Hotspur's name
Did seem defensible. So you left him.
Never, O never, do his ghost the wrong   40
To hold your honor more precise and nice
With others than with him! Let them alone.
The Marshal and the Archbishop are strong.

47. **Beshrew:** the devil take; a playful exclamation of irritation.

54. **Till that:** till; **commons:** common soldiers.

55. **Have of their puissance made a little taste:** have given some sign of their strength.

56. **get ground and vantage of:** secure an advantage over.

59. **for all our loves:** for the sake of us who love you.

61. **suffered:** indulged; allowed his will.

63. **rain upon remembrance with mine eyes:** i.e., weep on remembering.

65. **recordation to:** commemoration of.

70. **Fain would I go:** I would like to go.

73. **time and vantage:** an opportune time.

Had my sweet Harry had but half their numbers,
Today might I, hanging on Hotspur's neck,   45
Have talked of Monmouth's grave.
    North.   Beshrew your heart,
Fair daughter, you do draw my spirits from me
With new lamenting ancient oversights.
But I must go and meet with danger there,   50
Or it will seek me in another place
And find me worse provided.
    Wife.   O fly to Scotland,
Till that the nobles and the armed commons
Have of their puissance made a little taste.   55
    Lady P. If they get ground and vantage of the
        King,
Then join you with them, like a rib of steel,
To make strength stronger. But, for all our loves,
First let them try themselves. So did your son;   60
He was so suffered. So came I a widow,
And never shall have length of life enough
To rain upon remembrance with mine eyes,
That it may grow and sprout as high as heaven,
For recordation to my noble husband.   65
    North. Come, come; go in with me. 'Tis with my
        mind
As with the tide swelled up unto his height,
That makes a still-stand, running neither way.
Fain would I go to meet the Archbishop,   70
But many thousand reasons hold me back.
I will resolve for Scotland. There am I,
Till time and vantage crave my company.
                                    Exeunt.

II. iv. After carousing with Mistress Quickly, Falstaff and Doll Tearsheet are both tipsy. Pistol seeks admittance and Falstaff urges that he join the party; immediately, however, Doll and Pistol get into such a wrangle that Falstaff and Bardolph throw him out. Doll questions Falstaff about the Prince, and receives such an unflattering description that Hal, who is present in disguise, comes forward and reveals himself. Falstaff, defending himself, claims that he deliberately dispraised the Prince to prevent unworthy folk attaching themselves to him. At length, on Bardolph's urging, Falstaff sets out for York after sorrowful farewells to Doll and Mistress Quickly.

⁞⁞⁞⁞⁞⁞⁞⁞⁞⁞⁞⁞⁞⁞⁞⁞⁞⁞⁞⁞⁞⁞⁞⁞

2. **Applejohns:** apples which are not ripe until they appear withered.

10. **cover:** lay the cover (cloth).

11. **noise:** musicians.

14. **straight:** immediately.

19. **old utis:** a high old time; great fun. **Utis** is a variant form of "utas," which in turn is a reduced form of "octave," the eighth day of a festival, or, by extension, a period of festivity.

Scene IV. [The Boar's Head Tavern in Eastcheap.]

Enter a *Drawer* or *Two* [*Francis* and *Another*].

Fran. What the devil hast thou brought there?
Applejohns? Thou knowest Sir John cannot endure
an applejohn.

   2. Draw. Mass, thou sayest true. The Prince once
set a dish of applejohns before him, and told him   5
there were five more Sir Johns, and, putting off his
hat, said, "I will now take my leave of these six dry,
round, old, withered knights." It angered him to the
heart. But he hath forgot that.

   Fran. Why, then, cover, and set them down. And   10
see if thou canst find out Sneak's noise; Mistress Tearsheet would fain hear some music. Dispatch. The
room where they supped is too hot; they'll come in
straight.

Enter *Will* [a *Third Drawer*].

   3. Draw. Sirrah, here will be the Prince and Master   15
Poins anon, and they will put on two of our jerkins
and aprons, and Sir John must not know of it.
Bardolph hath brought word.   [*Exit.*]

   Fran. By the mass, here will be old utis. It will be
an excellent stratagem.   20

   2. Draw. I'll see if I can find out Sneak.   *Exit.*

23. **temperality:** physical condition; **pulsidge:** a malapropism for "pulse."

26. **canaries:** sweet wines.

27. **searching:** powerful.

30. **Hem:** this word has produced much commentary. Clearly Shakespeare meant merely to indicate a hiccup from tipsy Doll.

33-5. **"When . . . court," "And . . . king":** phrases from an old ballad, "Sir Launcelot du Lake."

34. **jordan:** chamberpot.

36. **calm:** qualm.

37-8. **sect:** sex; **An they be once in a calm, they are sick:** Falstaff puns on calm/qualm. "Women so love an uproar that they cannot endure a calm," he says.

39. **muddy:** dirty.

41. **fat rascals:** a quibble. In addition to the usual meaning of the word, **rascal** meant a lean deer; so Falstaff points out that he himself is too fat to be a **rascal.**

46. **poor virtue:** one of little virtue.

Enter *Mistress Quickly* and *Doll Tearsheet.*

Host. I' faith, sweetheart, methinks now you are in
an excellent good temperality. Your pulsidge beats as
extraordinarily as heart would desire, and your color,
I warrant you, is as red as any rose, in good truth, la!   25
But, i' faith, you have drunk too much canaries, and
that's a marvelous searching wine, and it perfumes the
blood ere one can say, "What's this?" How do you
now?

Doll. Better than I was. Hem!   30

Host. Why, that's well said. A good heart's worth
gold. Lo, here comes Sir John.

Enter *Sir John Falstaff.*

Fal. [*Sings*] "When Arthur first in court"—Empty
the jordan. [*Exit Francis.*]—[*Sings*] "And was a
worthy king."—How now, Mistress Doll!   35

Host. Sick of a calm, yea, good faith.

Fal. So is all her sect. An they be once in a calm,
they are sick.

Doll. A pox damn you, you muddy rascal, is that all
the comfort you give me?   40

Fal. You make fat rascals, Mistress Doll.

Doll. I make them! Gluttony and diseases make
them; I make them not.

Fal. If the cook help to make the gluttony, you
help to make the diseases, Doll. We catch of you,   45
Doll, we catch of you. Grant that, my poor virtue,
grant that.

49. **"Your brooches, pearls, and ouches"**: another fragment of a song, but Falstaff also means venereal sores.

52-3. **charged chambers**: loaded cannon, with a double meaning.

54. **conger**: conger eel, a frequenter of muddy waters.

58. **rheumatic**: touchy; irritable.

59. **confirmities**: infirmities.

60. **goodyear**: deuce.

64-5. **merchant's venture of Bordeaux stuff**: cargo of Bordeaux wines.

69. **Ancient**: ensign; standard-bearer.

Doll. Yea, joy, our chains and our jewels.

Fal. "Your brooches, pearls, and ouches." For to serve bravely is to come halting off, you know. To 50 come off the breach with his pike bent bravely, and to surgery bravely; to venture upon the charged chambers bravely—

Doll. Hang yourself, you muddy conger, hang yourself! 55

Host. By my troth, this is the old fashion. You two never meet but you fall to some discord. You are both, i' good truth, as rheumatic as two dry toasts; you cannot one bear with another's confirmities. What the goodyear! [*To Doll*] One must bear, and that must 60 be you; you are the weaker vessel, as they say, the emptier vessel.

Doll. Can a weak empty vessel bear such a huge full hogshead? There's a whole merchant's venture of Bordeaux stuff in him; you have not seen a hulk bet- 65 ter stuffed in the hold. Come, I'll be friends with thee, Jack. Thou art going to the wars, and whether I shall ever see thee again or no, there is nobody cares.

Enter *Drawer*.

Draw. Sir, Ancient Pistol's below and would speak with you. 70

Doll. Hang him, swaggering rascal! Let him not come hither. It is the foulmouthed'st rogue in England.

Host. If he swagger, let him not come here. No, by my faith. I must live among my neighbors, I'll no 75

84. **Tilly-fally:** fiddlesticks.

94-5. **swaggering companions:** roaring boys; rowdies.

97. **tame cheater:** swindler's decoy.

A courtesan.
From an old ballad.

swaggerers. I am in good name and fame with the
very best. Shut the door, there comes no swaggerers
here. I have not lived all this while to have swaggering now. Shut the door, I pray you.

Fal. Dost thou hear, hostess?   80

Host. Pray ye, pacify yourself, Sir John. There
comes no swaggerers here.

Fal. Dost thou hear? It is mine Ancient.

Host. Tilly-fally, Sir John, ne'er tell me. Your ancient swaggerer comes not in my doors. I was before   85
Master Tisick, the debuty, t' other day, and, as he said
to me—'twas no longer ago than Wednesday last—"I'
good faith, neighbor Quickly," says he—Master
Dumbe, our minister, was by then—"neighbor Quick-
ly," says he, "receive those that are civil, for," said he, 90
"you are in an ill name." Now 'a said so, I can tell
whereupon. "For," says he, "you are an honest woman, and well thought on; therefore take heed what
guests you receive. Receive," says he, "no swaggering
companions." There comes none here. You would   95
bless you to hear what he said. No, I'll no swaggerers.

Fal. He's no swaggerer, hostess; a tame cheater,
i' faith; you may stroke him as gently as a puppy
greyhound. He'll not swagger with a Barbary hen, if
her feathers turn back in any show of resistance. Call 100
him up, drawer.   [*Exit Drawer.*]

Host. Cheater, call you him? I will bar no honest
man my house, nor no cheater. But I do not love
swaggering, by my troth; I am the worse when one
says swagger. Feel, masters, how I shake; look you, I 105
warrant you.

111. **charge:** toast.

116. **offend:** injure.

123. **companion:** fellow, with a contemptuous connotation; see l. 95.

128. **cutpurse:** pickpocket. **Bung** is synonymous.

130. **chaps:** cheeks; **cuttle:** cutthroat.

131. **basket-hilt stale juggler:** i.e., one who flourishes a sword with a basket hilt pretending to be a valiant soldier.

132. **Since when:** Doll snorts at Pistol's pretensions to be a military man.

133. **points:** laces for fastening armor to the shoulders.

Doll. So you do, hostess.

Host. Do I? Yea, in very truth, do I, an 'twere an
aspen leaf. I cannot abide swaggerers.

Enter *Ancient Pistol, Bardolph,* and *Bardolph's Boy.*

Pist. God save you, Sir John!   110

Fal. Welcome, Ancient Pistol. Here, Pistol, I charge
you with a cup of sack. Do you discharge upon mine
hostess.

Pist. I will discharge upon her, Sir John, with two
bullets.   115

Fal. She is pistol-proof, sir; you shall hardly offend
her.

Host. Come, I'll drink no proofs nor no bullets. I'll
drink no more than will do me good, for no man's
pleasure, I.   120

Pist. Then to you, Mistress Dorothy; I will charge
you.

Doll. Charge me! I scorn you, scurvy companion.
What! You poor, base, rascally, cheating, lack-linen
mate! Away, you moldy rogue, away! I am meat for   125
your master.

Pist. I know you, Mistress Dorothy.

Doll. Away, you cutpurse rascal! You filthy bung,
away! By this wine, I'll thrust my knife in your moldy
chaps, an you play the saucy cuttle with me. Away, 130
you bottle-ale rascal! You basket-hilt stale juggler,
you! Since when, I pray you, sir? God's light, with
two points on your shoulder? Much!

142. **truncheon:** beat with a staff (**truncheon**).

146-47. **moldy stewed prunes and dried cakes:** leftovers found in bawdy houses. **Stewed prunes** were traditionally associated with houses of ill-fame, possibly because of belief in their medicinal virtues.

148-50. **as odious as the word "occupy," . . . sorted:** omitted from the Folio, probably because of the ribald allusion; **occupy:** slang for "copulate"; **was ill sorted:** fell into bad company.

157-58. **Pluto's damned lake:** i.e., the river Styx.

158. **Erebus:** the name of the classical underworld of impenetrable dark.

159. **Hold hook and line:** a proverbial saying: "Hold hook and line, then all is mine."

160. **Down . . . dogs:** probably a remembrance of lines from George Peele's *Battle of Alcazar* (1594): "Ye proud malicious dogs of Italy/Strike on, strike down this body to the earth"; **faitors:** impostors; cheats.

161. **Hiren:** a character in George Peele's play *The Turkish Mahomet and Hiren the Fair Greek* (c. 1594). The word later became synonymous with "harlot."

163. **aggravate:** moderate; another malapropism.

Pist. God let me not live but I will murder your ruff
for this.   135

Fal. No more, Pistol; I would not have you go off
here. Discharge yourself of our company, Pistol.

Host. No, good Captain Pistol, not here, sweet
Captain.

Doll. Captain! Thou abominable damned cheater, 140
art thou not ashamed to be called Captain? An captains were of my mind, they would truncheon you out
for taking their names upon you before you have
earned them. You a captain! You slave, for what? For
tearing a poor whore's ruff in a bawdyhouse? He a 145
captain! Hang him, rogue! He lives upon moldy
stewed prunes and dried cakes. A captain! God's light,
these villains will make the word as odious as the
word "occupy," which was an excellent good word
before it was ill sorted. Therefore captains had need 150
look to't.

Bar. Pray thee, go down, good Ancient.

Fal. Hark thee hither, Mistress Doll.

Pist. Not I. I tell thee what, Corporal Bardolph, I
could tear her. I'll be revenged of her.   155

Page. Pray thee, go down.

Pist. I'll see her damned first, to Pluto's damned
lake, by this hand, to the infernal deep, with Erebus
and tortures vile also. Hold hook and line, say I.
Down, down, dogs! Down, faitors! Have we not 160
Hiren here?

Host. Good Captain Peesel, be quiet; 'tis very late,
i' faith. I beseek you now, aggravate your choler.

166-67. **And . . . day:** a misquotation from Marlowe's *Tamburlaine.* Pistol is fond of ranting passages from contemporary drama, regardless of their relevance to the situation.

168. **Cannibals:** blunder for Hannibals.

169. **Trojan Greeks:** i.e., the Greeks who destroyed Troy.

170. **King Cerberus:** another blunder. Cerberus was the three-headed dog that guarded the entrance of Hades; **let the welkin roar:** a phrase from an old ballad. **Welkin** means heavens.

171. **fall foul:** fall out; conflict; **toys:** trifles. Perhaps he refers to Doll.

181. **feed . . . Calipolis:** another inaccurately recalled snatch from Peele's *Battle of Alcazar.*

183. **Si . . . contento:** Pistol quotes his own garbled version of a motto from Anthony Copley's *Wit's Fits and Fancies* (1595): *Si fortuna me tormenta, Il speranza me contenta.*

186. **points:** quibble on the sense "periods," and "sword points."

189. **neaf:** fist.

190. **seen the seven stars:** seen the Pleiades; i.e., spent many a night out, perhaps on the road as thieves.

192. **fustian:** bombastic, pretending much and meaning little.

Pist. These be good humors, indeed! Shall pack
    horses   165
And hollow pampered jades of Asia,
Which cannot go but thirty mile a day,
Compare with Cæsars, and with Cannibals,
And Trojan Greeks? Nay, rather damn them with
King Cerberus, and let the welkin roar.   170
Shall we fall foul for toys?

Host. By my troth, Captain, these are very bitter
words.

Bar. Be gone, good Ancient. This will grow to a
brawl anon.   175

Pist. Die men like dogs! Give crowns like pins!
Have we not Hiren here?

Host. O' my word, Captain, there's none such here.
What the goodyear! Do you think I would deny her?
For God's sake, be quiet.   180

Pist. Then feed, and be fat, my fair Calipolis.
Come, give's some sack.
Si *fortune me tormente, sperato me contento.*
Fear we broadsides? No, let the fiend give fire.
Give me some sack. And, sweetheart, lie thou there.   185
                              [*Lays down his sword.*]
Come we to full points here, and are etceteras no
    things?

Fal. Pistol, I would be quiet.

Pist. Sweet knight, I kiss thy neaf. What! We have
seen the seven stars.   190

Doll. For God's sake, thrust him downstairs. I cannot endure such a fustian rascal.

193-94. Galloway nags: common jades. In other words, Pistol protests at being thrust downstairs at the wish of Doll, a common whore.

195. Quoit: throw; **shovegroat:** a game similar to shuffleboard, played with coins.

199-200. incision: wounds; **imbrue:** shed blood.

201. death rock me asleep: a line from a poem sometimes attributed to Anne Boleyn.

203. the Sisters Three: the Fates, who decided the term of human life. **Atropos** was the one who cut the thread of life.

204. Here's a goodly stuff toward: fine doings we are likely to have now.

209. tirrits: disturbances.

215. shrewd: fierce.

Pist. Thrust him downstairs! Know we not Galloway nags?

Fal. Quoit him down, Bardolph, like a shovegroat   195
shilling. Nay, an 'a do nothing but speak nothing, 'a
shall be nothing here.

Bar. Come, get you downstairs.

Pist. What! shall we have incision? Shall we im-
brue?   [*Snatching up his sword.*]   200
Then death rock me asleep, abridge my doleful days!
Why then, let grievous, ghastly, gaping wounds
Untwine the Sisters Three! Come, Atropos, I say!

Host. Here's a goodly stuff toward!

Fal. Give me my rapier, boy.   205

Doll. I pray thee, Jack, I pray thee, do not draw.

Fal. Get you downstairs.

              [*Drawing, and driving Pistol out.*]

Host. Here's a goodly tumult! I'll forswear keeping
house afore I'll be in these tirrits and frights. So, murder, I warrant now. Alas, alas! Put up your naked   210
weapons, put up your naked weapons.

                 [*Exeunt Pistol and Bardolph*].

Doll. I pray thee, Jack, be quiet; the rascal's gone.
Ah, you whoreson little valiant villain, you!

Host. Are you not hurt i' the groin? Methought 'a
made a shrewd thrust at your belly.   215

[*Re-enter Bardolph.*]

Fal. Have you turned him out o' doors?

Bar. Yea, sir. The rascal's drunk. You have hurt
him, sir, i' the shoulder.

222. **chops:** fat-cheeks.

225. **the Nine Worthies:** popular figures in romance: Hector, Alexander, Julius Cæsar, Joshua, David, Judas Maccabaeus, King Arthur, Charlemagne, and Godfrey of Bouillon.

234-35. **like a church:** an obscure simile. Perhaps Doll means with persistence.

235-36. **tidy:** plump; **Bartholomew boar-pig:** a roast pig, such as were sold at Bartholomew Fair, a London fair held every year on St. Bartholomew's Day, August 24.

239-40. **death's-head:** skull, a traditional reminder of death often used in memorial rings.

241. **what humor's the Prince of:** i.e., what is the Prince's temperament.

Fal. A rascal! to brave me!

Doll. Ah, you sweet little rogue, you! Alas, poor 220
ape, how thou sweatest! Come, let me wipe thy face;
come on, you whoreson chops. Ah, rogue! i' faith, I
love thee. Thou art as valorous as Hector of Troy,
worth five of Agamemnon, and ten times better than
the Nine Worthies. Ah, villain!   225

Fal. A rascally slave! I will toss the rogue in a
blanket.

Doll. Do, an thou darest for thy heart. An thou
dost, I'll canvass thee between a pair of sheets.

Enter *Music.*

Page. The music is come, sir.   230

Fal. Let them play. Play, sirs. Sit on my knee, Doll.
A rascal bragging slave! The rogue fled from me like
quicksilver.

Doll. I' faith, and thou followedst him like a
church. Thou whoreson little tidy Bartholomew boar- 235
pig, when wilt thou leave fighting o' days and foining
o' nights, and begin to patch up thine old body for
heaven?

Enter *Prince* and *Poins* disguised.

Fal. Peace, good Doll! Do not speak like a death's-
head. Do not bid me remember mine end.   240

Doll. Sirrah, what humor's the Prince of?

Fal. A good shallow young fellow. 'A would have

243. **pantler:** pantryman; **chipped:** i.e., trimmed the crusts.

247. **Tewkesbury mustard:** Tewkesbury, a market town in Gloucestershire, was noted for its mustard.

248. **conceit:** inventive wit.

252. **drinks off candles' ends for flapdragons:** flapdragons was a game in which drinkers snatched raisins out of burning brandy and threw them blazing into their mouths. Poins has the nerve, apparently, to put out lighted candles in his mouth.

253. **wild mare:** a *double-entendre;* it can mean seesaw or it may be a contemptuous reference to a woman.

254. **joined-stools:** stools made by joiners, which were sturdier because of stretchers joining the legs.

255-56. **sign of the leg:** i.e., a bootmaker's sign; **bate:** discord.

257. **gambol:** playful.

260-61. **the weight of a hair will turn the scales between their avoirdupois:** i.e., they are equally lightweight fellows.

262. **nave of a wheel:** i.e., rotund "knave."

265-66. **whether the withered elder hath not his poll clawed like a parrot:** Doll is running her fingers through Falstaff's hair caressingly.

270. **Saturn and Venus:** that is, age and the goddess of love.

272. **the fiery Trigon, his man:** another allusion to Bardolph's fiery face. A **trigon** is a triangle formed by three signs of the zodiac; the **fiery Trigon** would be the signs of Aries, Leo, and Sagittarius.

49

made a good pantler; 'a would ha' chipped bread well.

Doll. They say Poins has a good wit. 245

Fal. He a good wit? Hang him, baboon! His wit's as thick as Tewkesbury mustard. There's no more conceit in him than is in a mallet.

Doll. Why does the Prince love him so, then?

Fal. Because their legs are both of a bigness, and 250 'a plays at quoits well, and eats conger and fennel, and drinks off candles' ends for flapdragons, and rides the wild mare with the boys, and jumps upon joined-stools, and swears with a good grace, and wears his boots very smooth, like unto the sign of the 255 leg, and breeds no bate with telling of discreet stories; and such other gambol faculties 'a has, that show a weak mind and an able body, for the which the Prince admits him. For the Prince himself is such another; the weight of a hair will turn the scales be- 260 tween their avoirdupois.

Prince. Would not this nave of a wheel have his ears cut off?

Poins. Let's beat him before his whore.

Prince. Look, whether the withered elder hath not 265 his poll clawed like a parrot.

Poins. Is it not strange that desire should so many years outlive performance?

Fal. Kiss me, Doll.

Prince. Saturn and Venus this year in conjunction! 270 What says the almanac to that?

Poins. And look whether the fiery Trigon, his man,

273-74. **tables, his notebook, his counsel-keeper:** i.e., the confidant of his bosom, Mistress Quickly.

275. **busses:** kisses.

281. **kirtle:** dress.

287. **hearken a' the end:** i.e., time will show my fidelity; see the previous use of this proverbial idea; II. ii. 47.

A tavern waiter.
From a seventeenth-century ballad.

be not lisping to his master's old tables, his notebook, his counsel-keeper.

Fal. Thou dost give me flattering busses.   275

Doll. By my troth, I kiss thee with a most constant heart.

Fal. I am old, I am old.

Doll. I love thee better than I love e'er a scurvy young boy of them all.   280

Fal. What stuff wilt have a kirtle of? I shall receive money o' Thursday. Shalt have a cap tomorrow. A merry song, come. It grows late; we'll to bed. Thou'lt forget me when I am gone.

Doll. By my troth, thou'lt set me a-weeping, an   285 thou sayest so. Prove that ever I dress myself handsome till thy return. Well, hearken a' the end.

Fal. Some sack, Francis.

Prince. ⎤
Poins. ⎦ Anon, anon, sir.   [*Coming forward.*]

Fal. Ha! a bastard son of the King's? And art not 290 thou Poins his brother?

Prince. Why, thou globe of sinful continents, what a life dost thou lead!

Fal. A better than thou. I am a gentleman; thou art a drawer.   295

Prince. Very true, sir, and I come to draw you out by the ears.

Host. O, the Lord preserve thy good Grace! By my troth, welcome to London. Now, the Lord bless that sweet face of thine! O Jesu, are you come from 300 Wales?

302. **compound of majesty:** product of royal union; royal offspring.

303. **this light flesh and corrupt blood:** i.e., Doll.

307-8. **take not the heat:** that is, allow your anger to cool. To act "in the heat" is the same as striking "while the iron is hot."

309. **candle-mine:** source of abundant tallow (fat).

320-21. **willful abuse:** deliberate disparagement.

Fal. Thou whoreson mad compound of majesty, by this light flesh and corrupt blood, thou art welcome.

Doll. How, you fat fool! I scorn you. 305

Poins. My lord, he will drive you out of your revenge and turn all to a merriment, if you take not the heat.

Prince. You whoreson candle-mine you, how vilely did you speak of me even now before this honest, 310 virtuous, civil gentlewoman!

Host. God's blessing of your good heart! And so she is, by my troth.

Fal. Didst thou hear me?

Prince. Yea, and you knew me, as you did when 315 you ran away by Gad's Hill. You knew I was at your back, and spoke it on purpose to try my patience.

Fal. No, no, no; not so. I did not think thou wast within hearing.

Prince. I shall drive you then to confess the willful 320 abuse, and then I know how to handle you.

Fal. No abuse, Hal, o' mine honor, no abuse.

Prince. Not to dispraise me and call me pantler and bread-chipper and I know not what?

Fal. No abuse, Hal. 325

Poins. No abuse?

Fal. No abuse, Ned, i' the world; honest Ned, none. I dispraised him before the wicked, that the wicked might not fall in love with him; in which doing, I have done the part of a careful friend and a 330 true subject, and thy father is to give me thanks for

336. **close:** contend; see previous use at II. i. 18.
340. **dead elm:** old man.
341. **pricked down:** marked; selected.
343. **maltworms:** tipplers; habitual ale-drinkers.
348. **burns:** causes to burn with venereal disease.
351. **quit:** acquitted.
353-54. **suffering flesh to be eaten in thy house, contrary to the law:** serving meat during Lent.
359-60. **His grace says that which his flesh rebels against:** that is, a spirit of grace inspires the Prince to call Doll a gentlewoman, a dignity which realistically he would deny her.

it. No abuse, Hal. None, Ned, none. No, faith, boys,
none.

Prince. See now, whether pure fear and entire
cowardice doth not make thee wrong this virtuous   335
gentlewoman to close with us. Is she of the wicked?
Is thine hostess here of the wicked? Or is thy boy of
the wicked? Or honest Bardolph, whose zeal burns
in his nose, of the wicked?

Poins. Answer, thou dead elm, answer.   340

Fal. The fiend hath pricked down Bardolph ir-
recoverable, and his face is Lucifer's privy-kitchen,
where he doth nothing but roast maltworms. For the
boy, there is a good angel about him, but the Devil
blinds him too.   345

Prince. For the women?

Fal. For one of them, she is in hell already, and
burns poor souls. For the other, I owe her money,
and whether she be damned for that, I know not.

Host. No, I warrant you.   350

Fal. No, I think thou art not. I think thou art quit
for that. Marry, there is another indictment upon
thee, for suffering flesh to be eaten in thy house, contrary to the law, for the which I think thou wilt howl.

Host. All victualers do so. What's a joint of mutton   355
or two in a whole Lent?

Prince. You, gentlewoman—

Doll. What says your Grace?

Fal. His grace says that which his flesh rebels
against.   *Peto knocks at door.*   360

Host. Who knocks so loud at door? Look to the
door there, Francis.

372-73. commotion: insurrection; **like the south/Borne with black vapor:** like the south wind, moving along with dark clouds.

Pistol's motto illustrated.
From John Denys, *Secrets of Angling* (1613).
(See II. iv. 159.)

Enter *Peto*.

Prince. Peto, how now! What news?

Peto. The King your father is at Westminster,
And there are twenty weak and wearied posts   365
Come from the north. And as I came along
I met and overtook a dozen captains,
Bareheaded, sweating, knocking at the taverns,
And asking every one for Sir John Falstaff.

Prince. By heaven, Poins, I feel me much to blame,   370
So idly to profane the precious time,
When tempest of commotion, like the south
Borne with black vapor, doth begin to melt
And drop upon our bare unarmed heads.
Give me my sword and cloak. Falstaff, good night.   375
     Exeunt Prince, Poins, [Peto, and Bardolph].

Fal. Now comes in the sweetest morsel of the
night, and we must hence and leave it unpicked.
[*Knocking within.*] More knocking at the door!

[Re-enter *Bardolph*.]

How now! What's the matter?

Bar. You must away to court, sir, presently.   380
A dozen captains stay at door for you.

Fal. [*To the Page*] Pay the musicians, sirrah. Farewell, hostess. Farewell, Doll. You see, my good
wenches, how men of merit are sought after. The un-

387. **post:** with all haste.

392. **come peasecod-time:** when peas next develop in the pod; i.e., late spring.

Pluto and his court, guarded by Cerberus.
From Natale Conti, *Mythologiae* (1616).
(See II. iv. 170.)

deserver may sleep when the man of action is called   385
on. Farewell, good wenches. If I be not sent away
post, I will see you again ere I go.

Doll. I cannot speak. If my heart be not ready to
burst—well, sweet Jack, have a care of thyself.

Fal. Farewell, farewell.   390

> *[Exeunt Falstaff and Bardolph.]*

Host. Well, fare thee well. I have known thee these
twenty-nine years, come peasecod-time, but an
honester and truer-hearted man—well, fare thee well.

Bar. [*Within*] Mistress Tearsheet!

Host. What's the matter?   395

Bar. [*Within*] Bid Mistress Tearsheet come to
my master.

Host. O, run, Doll, run. Run, good Doll. Come.
[*To Bardolph within*] She comes blubbered. Yea, will
you come, Doll?   400

> *Exeunt.*

THE HISTORY OF
HENRY
THE FOURTH
[PART 2]

ACT III

III. i. King Henry, in the middle of a sleepless night, confers with Warwick, Surrey, and Blunt about the new threat of rebellion. He remembers the prophecy of Richard II that Northumberland, who had betrayed his king in order to place Henry on the throne, would in time break his friendship with the new king. His friends believe that the latest rebellion will be easily crushed. The King once more expresses his longing to make a crusade to the Holy Land.

[This scene is altogether omitted from the first issue of the Quarto but is included in a variant issue, as well as in the Folio.]

‖‖‖‖‖‖‖‖‖‖‖‖‖‖‖‖‖‖‖‖‖‖‖‖‖‖‖

Ent. **nightgown:** dressing gown.

9. **cribs:** hovels.

10. **uneasy:** hard.

15. **thou dull god:** i.e., Morpheus, god of sleep.

17. **watchcase:** i.e., a place where the passing hours are noted.

ACT III

Scene I. [Westminster. The palace.]

Enter the King *in his nightgown, with a* Page.

King. Go call the Earls of Surrey and of Warwick.
But, ere they come, bid them o'erread these letters
And well consider of them. Make good speed.

          Exit [*Page*].

How many thousand of my poorest subjects
Are at this hour asleep! O sleep, O gentle sleep,   5
Nature's soft nurse, how have I frighted thee,
That thou no more wilt weigh my eyelids down
And steep my senses in forgetfulness?
Why rather, sleep, liest thou in smoky cribs,
Upon uneasy pallets stretching thee,   10
And hushed with buzzing night-flies to thy slumber,
Than in the perfumed chambers of the great,
Under the canopies of costly state,
And lulled with sound of sweetest melody?
O thou dull god, why liest thou with the vile   15
In loathsome beds, and leavest the kingly couch
A watchcase or a common 'larum-bell?
Wilt thou upon the high and giddy mast

20. **rude:** turbulent.

25. **hurly:** commotion.

26. **partial:** biased; i.e., showing special favor to some.

29. **appliances:** apparatuses; i.e., comfortable facilities; **to boot:** in addition.

30. **low:** lowly ones.

39. **foul:** loathsomely infected with disease; **rank:** festering.

41. **distempered:** disordered; sick.

46. **the revolution of the times:** the way time upsets everything.

Seal up the shipboy's eyes, and rock his brains
In cradle of the rude imperious surge   20
And in the visitation of the winds,
Who take the ruffian billows by the top,
Curling their monstrous heads and hanging them
With deafening clamor in the slippery clouds,
That, with the hurly, death itself awakes?   25
Canst thou, O partial sleep, give thy repose
To the wet seaboy in an hour so rude,
And in the calmest and most stillest night,
With all appliances and means to boot,
Deny it to a king? Then happy low, lie down!   30
Uneasy lies the head that wears a crown.

        Enter *Warwick, Surrey,* and *Sir John Blunt.*

  War. Many good morrows to your Majesty!
  King. Is it good morrow, lords?
  War. 'Tis one o'clock, and past.
  King. Why, then, good morrow to you all, my lords. 35
Have you read o'er the letters that I sent you?
  War. We have, my liege.
  King. Then you perceive the body of our kingdom
How foul it is; what rank diseases grow,
And with what danger, near the heart of it.   40
  War. It is but as a body yet distempered,
Which to his former strength may be restored
With good advice and little medicine.
My Lord Northumberland will soon be cooled.
  King. O God! that one might read the book of fate, 45
And see the revolution of the times

47. **continent:** earth; the dry parts of the globe.

50-1. **The beachy girdle of the ocean/Too wide for Neptune's hips:** Neptune, the sea god, is personified as the ocean and the shore that circles the ocean is compared with a girdle that becomes too big when the water recedes.

54. **through:** throughout; from beginning to end.

63. **under my foot:** loyally at my service.

64-5. **even to the eyes of Richard/Gave him defiance:** i.e., defied King Richard II to his face.

69. **checked and rated:** berated.

71-2, 76-8. **"Northumberland . . . throne,"** **"The . . . corruption":** these lines are adapted from Shakespeare's own *Richard II*, V. i. 55-9.

74-5. **necessity so bowed the state/That I and greatness were compelled to kiss:** conditions altered the state in such a way that greatness was thrust upon me.

77. **gathering head:** like a boil ready to break.

Make mountains level, and the continent,
Weary of solid firmness, melt itself
Into the sea! and other times to see
The beachy girdle of the ocean   50
Too wide for Neptune's hips; how chances mock,
And changes fill the cup of alteration
With divers liquors! O, if this were seen,
The happiest youth, viewing his progress through,
What perils past, what crosses to ensue,   55
Would shut the book, and sit him down and die.
'Tis not ten years gone
Since Richard and Northumberland, great friends,
Did feast together, and in two years after
Were they at wars. It is but eight years since   60
This Percy was the man nearest my soul,
Who like a brother toiled in my affairs
And laid his love and life under my foot,
Yea, for my sake, even to the eyes of Richard
Gave him defiance. But which of you was by—   65
[*To Warwick*] You, cousin Nevil, as I may
    remember—
When Richard, with his eye brimful of tears,
Then checked and rated by Northumberland,
Did speak these words, now proved a prophecy?   70
"Northumberland, thou ladder by the which
My cousin Bolingbroke ascends my throne"—
Though then, God knows, I had no such intent,
But that necessity so bowed the state
That I and greatness were compelled to kiss—   75
"The time shall come," thus did he follow it,
"The time will come that foul sin, gathering head,

82. **Figuring:** showing the form of; character-
izing.

88. **by the necessary form of this:** in accordance with the inevitably fixed principle already described.

106. **A certain instance:** reliable evidence.

Shall break into corruption." So went on,
Foretelling this same time's condition
And the division of our amity.   80

War. There is a history in all men's lives,
Figuring the nature of the times deceased,
The which observed, a man may prophesy,
With a near aim, of the main chance of things
As yet not come to life, which in their seeds   85
And weak beginnings lie intreasured.
Such things become the hatch and brood of time,
And by the necessary form of this
King Richard might create a perfect guess
That great Northumberland, then false to him,   90
Would of that seed grow to a greater falseness,
Which should not find a ground to root upon,
Unless on you.

King.   Are these things then necessities?
Then let us meet them like necessities.   95
And that same word even now cries out on us.
They say the Bishop and Northumberland
Are fifty thousand strong.

War.   It cannot be, my lord.
Rumor doth double, like the voice and echo,   100
The numbers of the feared. Please it your Grace
To go to bed. Upon my soul, my lord,
The powers that you already have sent forth
Shall bring this prize in very easily.
To comfort you the more, I have received   105
A certain instance that Glendower is dead.
Your Majesty hath been this fortnight ill,

108. **unseasoned hours:** i.e., keeping such unseasonable hours.

111. **inward:** internal; domestic.

||||||||||||||||||||||||||||||||||||||||||||||||||||||||||

III. ii. We are introduced to Justice Silence and Justice Shallow, one of Falstaff's old acquaintances, whose help Falstaff seeks in recruiting men for his company. The men Shallow produces are a sad lot, but since two of them are willing to buy their release, Falstaff finds the choice easy. Justice Shallow urges Falstaff to stay for dinner but he must be on his way. Observing that Shallow is a sucker ready for fleecing, Falstaff resolves to pay him a call when he returns from the war.

||||||||||||||||||||||||||||||||||||||

3. **rood:** cross.

5. **bedfellow:** wife.

8. **ousel:** blackbird; i.e., a brunet rather than fair.

13. **Inns o' Court:** i.e., to study law. The Inns of Court were legal societies that exercised the right of calling students to the bar. They got their special names from the buildings that they occupied.

And these unseasoned hours perforce must add
Unto your sickness.

    King.   I will take your counsel.   110
And were these inward wars once out of hand,
We would, dear lords, unto the Holy Land.

                                       Exeunt.

Scene II. [Gloucestershire. Before Justice Shallow's house.]

Enter Justice Shallow and Justice Silence with Mouldy, Shadow, Wart, Feeble, Bullcalf.

    Shal. Come on, come on, come on, sir. Give me
your hand, sir; give me your hand, sir; an early stirrer,
by the rood! And how doth my good cousin Silence?

    Sil. Good morrow, good cousin Shallow.

    Shal. And how doth my cousin, your bedfellow?   5
And your fairest daughter and mine, my goddaughter
Ellen?

    Sil. Alas, a black ousel, cousin Shallow!

    Shal. By yea and nay, sir, I dare say my cousin
William is become a good scholar. He is at Oxford   10
still, is he not?

    Sil. Indeed, sir, to my cost.

    Shal. 'A must, then, to the Inns o' Court shortly. I
was once of Clement's Inn, where I think they will
talk of mad Shallow yet.   15

18. **roundly:** wholeheartedly; with complete thoroughness.

21. **Cotswold:** i.e., from the Cotswold Hill country in Gloucestershire.

22. **swingebucklers:** swashbucklers.

23. **bona robas:** wanton women.

31. **crack:** young scamp.

39. **How:** how much is; what is the current price of.

45. **John a Gaunt:** Henry IV's father.

Sil. You were called "lusty Shallow" then, cousin.

Shal. By the mass, I was called anything. And I
would have done anything indeed too, and roundly
too. There was I, and little John Doit of Staffordshire,
and black George Barnes, and Francis Pickbone, and   20
Will Squele, a Cotswold man; you have not four such
swingebucklers in all the Inns o' Court again. And I
may say to you we knew where the bona robas were
and had the best of them all at commandment. Then
was Jack Falstaff, now Sir John, a boy, and page to   25
Thomas Mowbray, Duke of Norfolk.

Sil. This Sir John, cousin, that comes hither anon
about soldiers?

Shal. The same Sir John, the very same. I see him
break Skogan's head at the court-gate, when 'a was a   30
crack not thus high. And the very same day did I
fight with one Sampson Stockfish, a fruiterer, behind
Gray's Inn. Jesu, Jesu, the mad days that I have
spent! And to see how many of my old acquaintance
are dead!   35

Sil. We shall all follow, cousin.

Shal. Certain, 'tis certain; very sure, very sure.
Death, as the Psalmist saith, is certain to all; all shall
die. How a good yoke of bullocks at Stamford fair?

Sil. By my troth, I was not there.   40

Shal. Death is certain. Is old Double of your town
living yet?

Sil. Dead, sir.

Shal. Jesu, Jesu, dead! 'A drew a good bow, and
dead! 'A shot a fine shoot. John a Gaunt loved him   45
well and betted much money on his head. Dead! 'A

47. **clapped i' the clout at twelve score:** hit the target from twelve score yards away.

48-9. **carried you a forehand shaft a fourteen and a fourteen and a half:** shot an arrow in a straight line for a distance of 280 or 290 yards.

51. **Thereafter as they be:** according to their quality.

62. **tall:** brave, valorous.

64. **He greets me well:** i.e., it is a pleasure to have his greetings.

would have clapped i' the clout at twelve score, and
carried you a forehand shaft a fourteen and fourteen
and a half, that it would have done a man's heart
good to see. How a score of ewes now?   50

Sil. Thereafter as they be. A score of good ewes
may be worth ten pounds.

Shal. And is old Double dead?

Sil. Here comes two of Sir John Falstaff's men, as
I think.   55

Enter *Bardolph* and *One* with him.

Bar. Good morrow, honest gentleman. I beseech
you, which is Justice Shallow?

Shal. I am Robert Shallow, sir, a poor esquire of
this county, and one of the King's justices of the
peace. What is your good pleasure with me?   60

Bar. My captain, sir, commends him to you, my
captain, Sir John Falstaff, a tall gentleman, by heav-
en, and a most gallant leader.

Shal. He greets me well, sir. I knew him a good
backsword man. How doth the good knight? May I   65
ask how my lady his wife doth?

Bar. Sir, pardon, a soldier is better accommodated
than with a wife.

Shal. It is well said, in faith, sir, and it is well said
indeed too. Better accommodated! It is good, yea, in-   70
deed, is it. Good phrases are surely, and ever were,
very commendable. Accommodated! It comes of
accommodo. Very good, a good phrase.

Bar. Pardon me, sir. I have heard the word.

82. **just:** right.

84. **like well:** are in good condition.

88-9. **in commission with me:** a fellow member of the commission of the peace.

94. **sufficient:** able-bodied.

Archers and a halberdier.
From an old ballad.

Phrase call you it? By this good day, I know not the   75
phrase, but I will maintain the word with my sword
to be a soldier-like word, and a word of exceeding
good command, by heaven. Accommodated: that is,
when a man is, as they say, accommodated; or when
a man is, being, whereby 'a may be thought to be   80
accommodated, which is an excellent thing.

Enter *Sir John Falstaff.*

Shal. It is very just. Look, here comes good Sir
John. Give me your good hand, give me your worship's good hand. By my troth, you like well and bear
your years very well. Welcome, good Sir John.   85

Fal. I am glad to see you well, good Master Robert
Shallow. Master Surecard, as I think?

Shal. No, Sir John, it is my cousin Silence, in commission with me.

Fal. Good Master Silence, it well befits you should   90
be of the peace.

Sil. Your good worship is welcome.

Fal. Fie! This is hot weather, gentlemen. Have you
provided me here half a dozen sufficient men?

Shal. Marry, have we, sir. Will you sit?   95

Fal. Let me see them, I beseech you.

Shal. Where's the roll? Where's the roll? Where's
the roll? Let me see, let me see, let me see. So, so, so,
so, so, so, so. Yea, marry, sir. Ralph Mouldy! Let them
appear as I call; let them do so, let them do so. Let   100
me see, where is Mouldy?

Moul. Here, an't please you.

104. **friends:** relatives.
111. **Prick him:** mark him down.
113. **dame:** mother.
114. **husbandry:** farm chores.
117. **Go to:** that's enough; see II. ii. 37.
118. **spent:** gone.
131. **much:** i.e., not much.

Shal. What think you, Sir John? A good-limbed fellow, young, strong, and of good friends.

Fal. Is thy name Mouldy? 105

Moul. Yea, an't please you.

Fal. 'Tis the more time thou wert used.

Shal. Ha, ha, ha! most excellent, i' faith! Things that are moldy lack use. Very singular good! In faith, well said, Sir John, very well said. 110

Fal. Prick him.

Moul. I was pricked well enough before, an you could have let me alone. My old dame will be undone now for one to do her husbandry and her drudgery. You need not to have pricked me. There are other 115 men fitter to go out than I.

Fal. Go to. Peace, Mouldy; you shall go. Mouldy, it is time you were spent.

Moul. Spent!

Shal. Peace, fellow, peace. Stand aside. Know you 120 where you are? For the other, Sir John, let me see. Simon Shadow!

Fal. Yea, marry, let me have him to sit under. He's like to be a cold soldier.

Shal. Where's Shadow? 125

Shad. Here, sir.

Fal. Shadow, whose son art thou?

Shad. My mother's son, sir.

Fal. Thy mother's son! Like enough, and thy father's shadow. So the son of the female is the shadow 130 of the male. It is often so, indeed, but much of the father's substance!

Shal. Do you like him, Sir John?

135-36. shadows to fill up the muster book: mythical names of men for whom Falstaff could draw pay and rations.

144. were: would be.

145. stands: relies.

154. pricked you: pricked you out; dressed you up.

155. battle: army.

161. magnanimous: nobly valiant.

Fal. Shadow will serve for summer. Prick him, for we have a number of shadows to fill up the muster book. 135

Shal. Thomas Wart!

Fal. Where's he?

Wart. Here, sir.

Fal. Is thy name Wart? 140

Wart. Yea, sir.

Fal. Thou art a very ragged wart.

Shal. Shall I prick him, Sir John?

Fal. It were superfluous, for his apparel is built upon his back and the whole frame stands upon pins. 145 Prick him no more.

Shal. Ha, ha, ha! you can do it, sir, you can do it. I commend you well. Francis Feeble!

Fee. Here, sir.

Shal. What trade art thou, Feeble? 150

Fee. A woman's tailor, sir.

Shal. Shall I prick him, sir?

Fal. You may. But if he had been a man's tailor, he'd a' pricked you. Wilt thou make as many holes in an enemy's battle as thou hast done in a woman's 155 petticoat?

Fee. I will do my good will, sir. You can have no more.

Fal. Well said, good woman's tailor! Well said, courageous Feeble! Thou wilt be as valiant as the 160 wrathful dove or most magnanimous mouse. Prick the woman's tailor well, Master Shallow, deep, Master Shallow.

Fee. I would Wart might have gone, sir.

168. **thousands:** i.e., lice.

176. **likely:** promising.

185. **gown:** dressing gown, like an invalid.

192. **tarry:** stay for.

194. **since:** when.

195. **the Windmill:** an actual windmill existed in St. George's Field until the late eighteenth century, but Shakespeare may refer to a brothel known as the Windmill, which stood in Paris Garden, somewhat north of St. George's Field, a field near the Church of St. George the Martyr in Southwark.

Fal. I would thou wert a man's tailor, that thou 165
mightst mend him and make him fit to go. I cannot
put him to a private soldier that is the leader of so
many thousands. Let that suffice, most forcible
Feeble.

Fee. It shall suffice, sir. 170

Fal. I am bound to thee, reverend Feeble. Who is
next?

Shal. Peter Bullcalf o' the green!

Fal. Yea, marry, let's see Bullcalf.

Bull. Here, sir. 175

Fal. 'Fore God, a likely fellow! Come, prick me
Bullcalf till he roar again.

Bull. O Lord! good my lord Captain—

Fal. What, dost thou roar before thou art pricked?

Bull. O Lord, sir! I am a diseased man. 180

Fal. What disease hast thou?

Bull. A whoreson cold, sir, a cough, sir, which I
caught with ringing in the King's affairs upon his
coronation day, sir.

Fal. Come, thou shalt go to the wars in a gown. 185
We will have away thy cold, and I will take such
order that thy friends shall ring for thee. Is here all?

Shal. Here is two more called than your number.
You must have but four here, sir. And so, I pray you,
go in with me to dinner. 190

Fal. Come, I will go drink with you, but I cannot
tarry dinner. I am glad to see you, by my troth,
Master Shallow.

Shal. O Sir John, do you remember since we lay all
night in the Windmill in St. George's Field? 195

201. **away with:** endure.

218-19. **Hem, boys:** drink up, boys.

221. **Corporate:** Corporal.

222-23. **four Harry ten shillings in French crowns:** This is one of Shakespeare's many anachronisms. The Harry ten shillings, first issued by Henry VII, were worth five shillings at the time of the play, while a French crown was worth four shillings.

Fal. No more of that, good Master Shallow, no more of that.

Shal. Ha! 'Twas a merry night. And is Jane Nightwork alive?

Fal. She lives, Master Shallow.   200

Shal. She never could away with me.

Fal. Never, never, she would always say she could not abide Master Shallow.

Shal. By the mass, I could anger her to the heart. She was then a bona roba. Doth she hold her own 205 well?

Fal. Old, old, Master Shallow.

Shal. Nay, she must be old. She cannot choose but be old. Certain she's old, and had Robin Nightwork by old Nightwork before I came to Clement's Inn. 210

Sil. That's fifty-five year ago.

Shal. Ha, cousin Silence, that thou hadst seen that that this knight and I have seen! Ha, Sir John, said I well?

Fal. We have heard the chimes at midnight, 215 Master Shallow.

Shal. That we have, that we have, that we have; in faith, Sir John, we have. Our watchword was "Hem, boys!" Come, let's to dinner; come, let's to dinner. Jesus, the days that we have seen! Come, come.   220

          Exeunt [Falstaff and the Justices].

Bull. Good Master Corporate Bardolph, stand my friend, and here's four Harry ten shillings in French crowns for you. In very truth, sir, I had as lief be hanged, sir, as go. And yet for mine own part, sir, I do not care, but rather, because I am unwilling, and, 225

233. **forty:** probably forty shillings (two pounds). Bullcalf has given Bardolph a pound, and at ll. 244-45 Bardolph tells Falstaff that he has three pounds to free Mouldy and Bullcalf.

237. **so:** fine; well and good.

for mine own part, have a desire to stay with my friends. Else, sir, I did not care, for mine own part, so much.

Bar. Go to, stand aside.

Moul. And, good Master Corporal Captain, for my 230
old dame's sake, stand my friend. She has nobody to
do anything about her when I am gone, and she is
old, and cannot help herself. You shall have forty, sir.

Bar. Go to, stand aside.

Fee. By my troth, I care not. A man can die but 235
once. We owe God a death. I'll ne'er bear a base
mind. An't be my destiny, so; an't be not, so. No man
is too good to serve's prince. And let it go which way
it will, he that dies this year is quit for the next.

Bar. Well said. Th' art a good fellow. 240

Fee. Faith, I'll bear no base mind.

Enter *Falstaff* and the *Justices*.

Fal. Come, sir, which men shall I have?

Shal. Four of which you please.

Bar. Sir, a word with you. I have three pound to
free Mouldy and Bullcalf. 245

Fal. Go to, well.

Shal. Come, Sir John, which four will you have?

Fal. Do you choose for me.

Shal. Marry, then, Mouldy, Bullcalf, Feeble, and
Shadow. 250

Fal. Mouldy and Bullcalf. For you, Mouldy, stay
at home till you are past service. And for your part,

259. **thews:** strength.

260. **assemblance:** semblance; show.

262-64. **charge you and discharge you:** load and fire; **with the motion of a pewterer's hammer:** i.e., rapidly and steadily.

264. **gibbets:** hangs.

265. **bucket:** a yoke to fit a man's shoulders. Heavy objects could be attached to each end; **half-faced fellow:** i.e., the profile of a man only. Shadow, in keeping with his name, is comically thin.

267. **with as great aim level:** with as large a target aim; i.e., have as large a target to aim at.

271. **caliver:** musket.

272. **traverse:** march back and forth.

275. **chopped:** chapped; **Well said:** well done.

276. **scab:** i.e., "Wart"; **tester:** a sixpence, from the French *teston*.

280-81. **Sir Dagonet:** fool to King Arthur in the Arthurian legend; **Arthur's show:** an annual exhibition of archery given in the city of London.

281. **quiver:** active; quick.

Bullcalf, grow till you come unto it. I will none of
you.

   Shal. Sir John, Sir John, do not yourself wrong. 255
They are your likeliest men, and I would have you
served with the best.

   Fal. Will you tell me, Master Shallow, how to
choose a man? Care I for the limb, the thews, the
stature, bulk, and big assemblance of a man! Give me 260
the spirit, Master Shallow. Here's Wart. You see what
a ragged appearance it is. 'A shall charge you and
discharge you with the motion of a pewterer's hammer, come off and on swifter than he that gibbets on
the brewer's bucket. And this same half-faced fellow, 265
Shadow: give me this man. He presents no mark to
the enemy; the foeman may with as great aim level
at the edge of a penknife. And for a retreat, how
swiftly will this Feeble the woman's tailor run off!
O give me the spare men, and spare me the great 270
ones. Put me a caliver into Wart's hand, Bardolph.

   Bar. Hold, Wart, traverse. Thus, thus, thus.

   Fal. Come, manage me your caliver. So. Very well!
Go to. Very good, exceeding good. O give me always
a little, lean, old, chopped, bald shot. Well said, i' 275
faith, Wart. Th' art a good scab. Hold, there's a tester
for thee.

   Shal. He is not his craft's master, he doth not do it
right. I remember at Mile-end Green, when I lay at
Clement's Inn—I was then Sir Dagonet in Arthur's 280
show—there was a little quiver fellow, and 'a would
manage you his piece thus, and 'a would about and
about, and come you in and come you in. "Rah, tah,

284. **Bounce:** an imitation of the sound of a musket's discharge.

297. **Go to, I have spoke at a word:** I have said my say. Shallow probably means that his word is as good as his deed.

300. **fetch off:** "take"; fleece.

305. **Turnbull Street:** a red-light district, a neighborhood of whores and toughs.

306-7. **duer paid to the hearer than the Turk's tribute:** duer equals "more duly" or more promptly. The sultan of Turkey demanded regular payments of money for protection against his pirates.

311. **forlorn:** meager.

312. **to any thick sight:** to anyone of poor vision; **invincible:** invisible.

313. **genius:** embodiment.

314. **mandrake:** see I. [ii.] 15.

tah," would 'a say, "Bounce," would 'a say, and away
again would 'a go, and again would 'a come. I shall 285
ne'er see such a fellow.

   Fal. These fellows will do well, Master Shallow.
God keep you, Master Silence. I will not use many
words with you: fare you well, gentlemen both. I
thank you. I must a dozen mile tonight. Bardolph, 290
give the soldiers coats.

   Shal. Sir John, the Lord bless you! God prosper
your affairs! God send us peace! At your return visit
our house, let our old acquaintance be renewed. Per-
adventure I will with ye to the court.   295

   Fal. 'Fore God, would you would, Master Shallow.

   Shal. Go to, I have spoke at a word. God keep you.

   Fal. Fare you well, gentle gentlemen. *(Exeunt [Jus-
tices].)* On, Bardolph, lead the men away. *[Exeunt
Bardolph and recruits.]* As I return, I will fetch off 300
these justices. I do see the bottom of Justice Shallow.
Lord, Lord, how subject we old men are to this vice
of lying! This same starved justice hath done nothing
but prate to me of the wildness of his youth and the
feats he hath done about Turnbull Street, and every 305
third word a lie, duer paid to the hearer than the
Turk's tribute. I do remember him at Clement's Inn
like a man made after supper of a cheese paring.
When 'a was naked, he was for all the world like a
forked radish, with a head fantastically carved upon 310
it with a knife. 'A was so forlorn that his dimensions
to any thick sight were invincible. 'A was the very
genius of famine, yet lecherous as a monkey, and the
whores called him mandrake. 'A came ever in the

316. **overscutched:** broken-down; decrepit; **hus-wifes:** hussies; whores; **carmen:** wagon drivers.

317-18. **fancies:** love songs; **good nights:** serenades; **Vice's dagger:** another allusion to Shallow's physique; the Vice was a comic character in morality plays who often carried a dagger with which he beat the Devil.

323-24. **his own name:** i.e., Gaunt.

325. **hautboy:** oboe.

328-29. **'t shall go hard but I will:** I shall, unless insuperable obstacles prevent; **a philosopher's two stones:** i.e., a source of wealth; **dace:** a small fish.

An alchemist, seeking the philosopher's stone.
From Konrad Gesner, *The Practice of the New and Old Physic* (1599).

rearward of the fashion, and sung those tunes to the 315
overscutched huswives that he heard the carmen
whistle, and sware they were his fancies or his good
nights. And now is this Vice's dagger become a
squire, and talks as familiarly of John a Gaunt as if he
had been sworn brother to him, and I'll be sworn 'a 320
ne'er saw him but once in the Tiltyard, and then he
burst his head for crowding among the Marshal's
men. I saw it, and told John a Gaunt he beat his own
name, for you might have thrust him and all his apparel into an eelskin; the case of a treble hautboy 325
was a mansion for him, a court. And now has he land
and beefs. Well, I'll be acquainted with him, if I return, and 't shall go hard but I will make him a
philosopher's two stones to me. If the young dace be
a bait for the old pike, I see no reason in the law of 330
nature but I may snap at him. Let time shape, and
there an end.

Exit.

THE HISTORY OF
HENRY
THE FOURTH
[PART 2]

ACT IV

IV. i. Shortly after the Archbishop of York and his fellow rebels have heard that Northumberland will not join them, Westmoreland comes to negotiate on behalf of the King. He offers the King's promise of mercy and attention to their grievances. Although Mowbray, son of an old enemy of the King, advises against surrender without a battle, the Archbishop favors the meeting with Prince John proposed by Westmoreland.

‖‖‖‖‖‖‖‖‖‖‖‖‖‖‖‖‖‖‖‖‖‖‖‖‖‖‖

4. **discoverers:** explorers; i.e., scouts.

13-5. **Here . . . levy:** i.e., he wishes he could be here himself accompanied by forces of suitable rank, but he has been unable to raise such forces.

19. **opposite:** opposition; enemy.

ACT IV

Scene I. [Yorkshire. Gaultree Forest.]

Enter the *Archbishop* [*of York*], *Mowbray, Hastings,*
[and *Others*], within the Forest of Gaultree.

Arch. What is this forest called?

Hast. 'Tis Gaultree Forest, an't shall please your
Grace.

Arch. Here stand, my lords, and send discoverers
forth   5
To know the numbers of our enemies.

Hast. We have sent forth already.

Arch.   'Tis well done.
My friends and brethren in these great affairs,
I must acquaint you that I have received   10
New-dated letters from Northumberland,
Their cold intent, tenor, and substance, thus:
Here doth he wish his person, with such powers
As might hold sortance with his quality,
The which he could not levy. Whereupon   15
He is retired, to ripe his growing fortunes,
To Scotland, and concludes in hearty prayers
That your attempts may overlive the hazard
And fearful meeting of their opposite.

25. **form:** array.

28. **just proportion that we gave them out:** exact number we had guessed.

29. **sway:** move.

30. **fronts:** confronts.

39. **in base and abject routs:** in the form of mobs of mean and despicable citizens.

40. **guarded:** trimmed; **rags:** the Folio and Quarto texts read "rage." The reading **rags,** suggested by early editors, has been adopted by most subsequent editors, but "rage" is possibly correct.

41. **countenanced:** supported.

42. **commotion:** rebellion; as at II. iv. 372.

45. **dress:** trim; embellish.

Mow. Thus do the hopes we have in him touch   20
    ground
And dash themselves to pieces.

Enter *Messenger*.

Hast.   Now, what news?
Mess. West of this forest, scarcely off a mile,
In goodly form comes on the enemy,   25
And, by the ground they hide, I judge their number
Upon or near the rate of thirty thousand.
Mow. The just proportion that we gave them out.
Let us sway on and face them in the field.
Arch. What well-appointed leader fronts us here? 30

Enter *Westmoreland*.

Mow. I think it is my Lord of Westmoreland.
West. Health and fair greeting from our general,
The prince, Lord John and Duke of Lancaster.
Arch. Say on, my Lord of Westmoreland, in peace.
What doth concern your coming?   35
West.   Then, my lord,
Unto your Grace do I in chief address
The substance of my speech. If that rebellion
Came like itself, in base and abject routs,
Led on by bloody youth, guarded with rags,   40
And countenanced by boys and beggary—
I say, if damned commotion so appeared,
In his true, native and most proper shape,
You, reverend father, and these noble lords
Had not been here, to dress the ugly form   45

51. **investments:** vestments; **figure:** symbolize.

53. **translate:** convert.

58. **point of war:** martial signal sounded on a trumpet.

61-86. **And . . . wrong:** from the Folio; omitted from the Quarto.

61. **surfeiting and wanton:** excessively self-indulgent.

63. **bleed:** shed blood in battle, as a patient is bled by his physician.

66. **take not on me here as:** do not assume here the role of.

69. **show:** appear.

70. **rank:** swollen with indulgence.

76. **griefs:** grievances.

Of base and bloody insurrection
With your fair honors. You, Lord Archbishop,
Whose see is by a civil peace maintained,
Whose beard the silver hand of peace hath touched,
Whose learning and good letters peace hath tutored,   50
Whose white investments figure innocence,
The dove and very blessed spirit of peace,
Wherefore do you so ill translate yourself
Out of the speech of peace that bears such grace,
Into the harsh and boisterous tongue of war,   55
Turning your books to graves, your ink to blood,
Your pens to lances, and your tongue divine
To a loud trumpet and a point of war?
    Arch. Wherefore do I this? So the question stands.
Briefly to this end: we are all diseased,   60
And with our surfeiting and wanton hours
Have brought ourselves into a burning fever,
And we must bleed for it. Of which disease
Our late King, Richard, being infected, died.
But, my most noble Lord of Westmoreland,   65
I take not on me here as a physician,
Nor do I as an enemy to peace
Troop in the throngs of military men,
But rather show awhile like fearful war,
To diet rank minds sick of happiness   70
And purge the obstructions which begin to stop
Our very veins of life. Hear me more plainly.
I have in equal balance justly weighed
What wrongs our arms may do, what wrongs we
    suffer,   75
And find our griefs heavier than our offenses.

78. **our most quiet there:** my most tranquil period of life, old age.

90. **Of every minute's instance:** happening every minute.

91. **ill-beseeming:** ill-becoming; unsuitable.

94. **Concurring both in name and quality:** i.e., actual peace, not peace in name only.

96. **galled:** injured.

97. **suborned:** evilly induced; **grate on:** harass.

98-9. **book/Of forged rebellion:** i.e., a brief of the falsely contrived grievances by which the rebellion is justified.

101. **brother general:** i.e., the commonwealth.

102. **To brother born an household cruelty:** this is an obscure line that no editor has succeeded in clarifying. It appears to refer to the internecine quarrels in the state. This line and l. 100, "And . . . edge," were omitted from the Folio and some copies of the Quarto. Apparently a passage was lost or garbled at this point.

We see which way the stream of time doth run,
And are enforced from our most quiet there
By the rough torrent of occasion;
And have the summary of all our griefs,   80
When time shall serve, to show in articles,
Which long ere this we offered to the King,
And might by no suit gain our audience.
When we are wronged and would unfold our griefs,
We are denied access unto his person   85
Even by those men that most have done us wrong.
The dangers of the days but newly gone,
Whose memory is written on the earth
With yet appearing blood, and the examples
Of every minute's instance, present now,   90
Hath put us in these ill-beseeming arms,
Not to break peace or any branch of it,
But to establish here a peace indeed,
Concurring both in name and quality.

    West. When ever yet was your appeal denied?   95
Wherein have you been galled by the King?
What peer hath been suborned to grate on you,
That you should seal this lawless bloody book
Of forged rebellion with a seal divine
And consecrate commotion's bitter edge?   100

    Arch. My brother general, the commonwealth,
To brother born an household cruelty,
I make my quarrel in particular.

    West. There is no need of any such redress,
Or if there were, it not belongs to you.   105

    Mow. Why not to him in part, and to us all
That feel the bruises of the days before,

109. **unequal:** unjust.

111-50. **O . . . King:** from the Folio; omitted from the Quarto.

112. **to:** i.e., according to.

119. **seignories:** dominions.

122. **breathed:** almost synonymous with **revived;** freshly endowed with breath.

124. **force perforce:** willy-nilly.

126. **roused:** raised.

127. **daring of the spur:** i.e., prompting their neighing horses with the spur.

128. **staves:** lances; **in charge:** poised to charge; **beavers:** helmet visors.

129. **sights:** i.e., the slits in their visors.

131-35. **Then . . . threw:** Shakespeare pictures the encounter between Norfolk and Hereford in *Richard II*, I. iii. In accordance with Holinshed, King Richard II halted the fight before either knight had come close to the other.

134. **warder:** a staff used by the presiding official to signal the beginning and end of engagement in a battle or tournament.

137. **indictment:** legal process.

138. **miscarried:** died.

And suffer the condition of these times
To lay a heavy and unequal hand
Upon our honors?   110
   West.   O my good Lord Mowbray,
Construe the times to their necessities,
And you shall say indeed, it is the time,
And not the King, that doth you injuries.
Yet for your part, it not appears to me   115
Either from the King or in the present time
That you should have an inch of any ground
To build a grief on. Were you not restored
To all the Duke of Norfolk's seignories,
Your noble and right well remembered father's?   120
   Mow. What thing, in honor, had my father lost,
That need to be revived and breathed in me?
The king that loved him, as the state stood then,
Was force perforce compelled to banish him.
And then that Henry Bolingbroke and he,   125
Being mounted and both roused in their seats,
Their neighing coursers daring of the spur,
Their armed staves in charge, their beavers down,
Their eyes of fire sparkling through sights of steel,
And the loud trumpet blowing them together,   130
Then, then, when there was nothing could have
    stayed
My father from the breast of Bolingbroke,
O, when the King did throw his warder down,
His own life hung upon the staff he threw.   135
Then threw he down himself and all their lives
That by indictment and by dint of sword
Have since miscarried under Bolingbroke.

141. **Earl of Hereford:** the title at that time of Bolingbroke, now Henry IV.

146. **Coventry:** site of the combat.

156. **set off:** discounted.

160. **overween:** are too self-confident.

162. **ken:** kenning, a marine measure of about 20-21 miles, being the ordinary range of human vision at sea.

168. **reason will:** i.e., reason will have it that; it is only reasonable that.

West. You speak, Lord Mowbray, now you know
 not what.   140
The Earl of Hereford was reputed then
In England the most valiant gentleman.
Who knows on whom fortune would then have
 smiled?
But if your father had been victor there,   145
He ne'er had borne it out of Coventry;
For all the country in a general voice
Cried hate upon him, and all their prayers and love
Were set on Hereford, whom they doted on
And blessed and graced indeed, more than the King. 150
But this is mere digression from my purpose.
Here come I from our princely general
To know your griefs, to tell you from his Grace
That he will give you audience, and wherein
It shall appear that your demands are just,   155
You shall enjoy them, everything set off
That might so much as think you enemies.

 Mow. But he hath forced us to compel this offer,
And it proceeds from policy, not love.

 West. Mowbray, you overween to take it so.   160
This offer comes from mercy, not from fear.
For, lo! within a ken our army lies,
Upon mine honor, all too confident
To give admittance to a thought of fear.
Our battle is more full of names than yours,   165
Our men more perfect in the use of arms,
Our armor all as strong, our cause the best:
Then reason will our hearts should be as good.
Say you not then our offer is compelled.

172. **rotten:** unsound.

174. **In very ample virtue of his father:** with his father's full power behind him.

177. **intended:** indicated.

178. **muse:** wonder that.

184. **insinewed:** joined as with strong tendons.

185. **Acquitted:** satisfied. The whole passage may be paraphrased: If all of the grievances set forth herein are dealt with, and everyone involved in our cause satisfied by a firm agreement and instant action to effect the ends we wish to achieve, then we will return to our proper places and support peaceful pursuits.

188. **We come within our awful banks again:** we shall return to our own confines and show due reverence for the King's authority. The metaphor pictures the rebels as comparable to a torrential river that has burst its banks.

194. **place of difference:** battlefield.

Mow. Well, by my will we shall admit no parley. 170
West. That argues but the shame of your offense.
A rotten case abides no handling.
Hast. Hath the Prince John a full commission,
In very ample virtue of his father,
To hear and absolutely to determine   175
Of what conditions we shall stand upon?
West. That is intended in the general's name.
I muse you make so slight a question.
Arch. Then take, my Lord of Westmoreland, this
    schedule,   180
For this contains our general grievances.
Each several article herein redressed,
All members of our cause, both here and hence,
That are insinewed to this action,
Acquitted by a true substantial form   185
And present execution of our wills
To us and to our purposes confined,
We come within our awful banks again
And knit our powers to the arm of peace.
West. This will I show the general. Please you, 190
    lords,
In sight of both our battles we may meet,
And either end in peace—which God so frame—
Or to the place of difference call the swords
Which must decide it.   195
Arch.   My lord, we will do so.
                              Exit Westmoreland.
Mow. There is a thing within my bosom tells me
That no conditions of our peace can stand.
Hast. Fear you not that. If we can make our peace

201. **consist:** stand; insist.

205. **nice:** trivial; **wanton:** capricious.

207. **were our royal faiths martyrs in love:** even if we were martyrs because of our devotion to the King.

212. **dainty and such picking:** such finicky and trifling.

213. **doubt:** object of fear.

214. **heirs of life:** survivors; living heirs of the victim.

215. **tables:** notebook; see II. iv. 273.

219. **precisely:** entirely.

220. **misdoubts present occasion:** fears show cause.

227. **hangs:** suspends.

Upon such large terms and so absolute   200
As our conditions shall consist upon,
Our peace shall stand as firm as rocky mountains.
  Mow. Yea, but our valuation shall be such
That every slight and false-derived cause,
Yea, every idle, nice, and wanton reason,   205
Shall to the King taste of this action;
That, were our royal faiths martyrs in love,
We shall be winnowed with so rough a wind
That even our corn shall seem as light as chaff
And good from bad find no partition.   210
  Arch. No, no, my lord. Note this: the King is weary
Of dainty and such picking grievances;
For he hath found to end one doubt by death
Revives two greater in the heirs of life,
And therefore will he wipe his tables clean   215
And keep no telltale to his memory
That may repeat and history his loss
To new remembrance. For full well he knows
He cannot so precisely weed this land
As his misdoubts present occasion.   220
His foes are so enrooted with his friends
That, plucking to unfix an enemy,
He doth unfasten so and shake a friend.
So that this land, like an offensive wife
That hath enraged him on to offer strokes,   225
As he is striking, holds his infant up
And hangs resolved correction in the arm
That was upreared to execution.
  Hast. Besides, the King hath wasted all his rods
On late offenders, that he now doth lack   230

233. **offer, but not hold:** offer a threat that it cannot carry out.

236. **atonement:** reconciliation.

243. **just distance 'tween:** i.e., halfway between.

The very instruments of chastisement.
So that his power, like to a fangless lion,
May offer, but not hold.
   Arch.   'Tis very true.
And therefore be assured, my good Lord Marshal,   235
If we do now make our atonement well,
Our peace will, like a broken limb united,
Grow stronger for the breaking.
   Mow.   Be it so.
Here is returned my Lord of Westmoreland.   240

Enter *Westmoreland.*

   West. The prince is here at hand. Pleaseth your
     lordship
To meet his Grace just distance 'tween our armies.
   Mow. Your Grace of York, in God's name then,
     set forward.   245
   Arch. Before, and greet his Grace, my lord; we
     come.
                                  [Exeunt.]

IV. [**ii.**] Prince John promises that the rebels' grievances will receive attention and persuades the Archbishop to dismiss his troops. Immediately after the Archbishop's compliance he orders the arrest of the Archbishop and his officers and their speedy execution for treason.

<hr>

5. **it better showed with you:** you appeared to better advantage.

9. **an iron man:** i.e., armored for battle.

14. **countenance:** patronage; see **countenanced** at IV. i. 41.

15. **set abroach:** let loose; the metaphor refers to opening the tap of a keg and allowing the drink to flow freely.

21. **opener and intelligencer:** reporter and messenger.

23. **workings:** i.e., actions of our consciences.

[Scene II. Another part of Gaultree Forest.]

Enter, [from one side, *Mowbray,* attended;
afterwards the *Archbishop, Hastings,* and *Others:*
from the other side,] *Prince John* and his *Army*
                   [and *Westmoreland*].

John. You are well encountered here, my cousin
    Mowbray.
Good day to you, gentle Lord Archbishop.
And so to you, Lord Hastings, and to all.
My Lord of York, it better showed with you   5
When that your flock, assembled by the bell,
Encircled you to hear with reverence
Your exposition on the holy text,
Than now to see you here an iron man,
Cheering a rout of rebels with your drum,   10
Turning the word to sword and life to death.
That man that sits within a monarch's heart
And ripens in the sunshine of his favor,
Would he abuse the countenance of the king,
Alack, what mischiefs might he set abroach   15
In shadow of such greatness. With you, Lord Bishop,
It is even so. Who hath not heard it spoken
How deep you were within the books of God?
To us the speaker in His Parliament,
To us the imagined voice of God himself,   20
The very opener and intelligencer
Between the grace, the sanctities of heaven
And our dull workings. O, who shall believe

27. **ta'en up:** enlisted.

31. **upswarmed:** gathered in a throng.

36. **monstrous:** unnatural (being clad in armor).

38. **parcels:** details.

41. **Hydra:** the many-headed serpent killed by Hercules; i.e., something difficult to overcome.

42. **Whose dangerous eyes may well be charmed asleep:** Shakespeare apparently is confusing Hydra with Argus, the hundred-eyed monster who was lulled to sleep by Hermes' music.

45. **Stoop:** bow in submission.

49. **supplies:** reinforcements; see I. [iii.] 13.

51. **success of mischief shall be born:** one trouble shall succeed the other.

53. **generation:** offspring.

But you misuse the reverence of your place,
Employ the countenance and grace of heaven,   25
As a false favorite doth his prince's name,
In deeds dishonorable? You have ta'en up,
Under the counterfeited zeal of God,
The subjects of His substitute, my father,
And both against the peace of heaven and him   30
Have here upswarmed them.
    Arch.   Good my Lord of Lancaster,
I am not here against your father's peace,
But, as I told my Lord of Westmoreland,
The time misordered doth, in common sense,   35
Crowd us and crush us to this monstrous form,
To hold our safety up. I sent your Grace
The parcels and particulars of our grief,
The which hath been with scorn shoved from the
        court,   40
Whereon this Hydra son of war is born,
Whose dangerous eyes may well be charmed asleep
With grant of our most just and right desires,
And true obedience, of this madness cured,
Stoop tamely to the foot of majesty.   45
    Mow. If not, we ready are to try our fortunes
To the last man.
    Hast.   And though we here fall down,
We have supplies to second our attempt.
If they miscarry, theirs shall second them,   50
And so success of mischief shall be born
And heir from heir shall hold this quarrel up
Whiles England shall have generation.

59. **allow:** accept as satisfactory.
62. **lavishly:** freely.
63. **Wrested:** distorted.
75. **part:** depart.
76. **Hie:** hurry.

Hercules and the Hydra.
From Guillaume de La Perrière, *Le théâtre des bon engins* (1539).

John. You are too shallow, Hastings, much too
    shallow,   55
To sound the bottom of the aftertimes.
    West. Pleaseth your Grace to answer them directly
How far forth you do like their articles.
    John. I like them all, and do allow them well,
And swear here, by the honor of my blood,   60
My father's purposes have been mistook,
And some about him have too lavishly
Wrested his meaning and authority.
My lord, these griefs shall be with speed redressed,
Upon my soul, they shall. If this may please you,   65
Discharge your powers unto their several counties,
As we will ours. And here between the armies
Let's drink together friendly and embrace,
That all their eyes may bear those tokens home
Of our restored love and amity.   70
    Arch. I take your princely word for these redresses.
    John. I give it you, and will maintain my word.
And thereupon I drink unto your Grace.
    Hast. Go, Captain, and deliver to the army
This news of peace. Let them have pay, and part.   75
I know it will well please them. Hie thee, Captain.
                                        Exit [Officer].
    Arch. To you, my noble Lord of Westmoreland.
    West. I pledge your Grace, and, if you knew what
    pains
I have bestowed to breed this present peace,   80
You would drink freely. But my love to ye
Shall show itself more openly hereafter.
    Arch. I do not doubt you.

87. **something:** somewhat.
88. **Against:** in anticipation of; before.
89. **heaviness:** sorrow; see I. [i.] 137.
93. **passing:** exceedingly.
95. **rendered:** stated.
105. **coped withal:** encountered in battle.

West.   I am glad of it.
Health to my lord and gentle cousin, Mowbray.   85
   Mow. You wish me health in very happy season,
For I am, on the sudden, something ill.
   Arch. Against ill chances men are ever merry,
But heaviness foreruns the good event.
   West. Therefore be merry, coz, since sudden sorrow   90
Serves to say thus, "Some good thing comes to-
   morrow."
   Arch. Believe me, I am passing light in spirit.
   Mow. So much the worse, if your own rule be true.
                             Shouts [*within*].
   John. The word of peace is rendered. Hark, how   95
   they shout!
   Mow. This had been cheerful after victory.
   Arch. A peace is of the nature of a conquest,
For then both parties nobly are subdued,
And neither party loser.   100
   John.   Go, my lord,
And let our army be discharged too.
                        [*Exit Westmoreland*].
And, good my lord, so please you, let our trains
March by us, that we may peruse the men
We should have coped withal.   105
   Arch.   Go, good Lord Hastings,
And, ere they be dismissed, let them march by.
                             Exit [*Hastings*].
   John. I trust, lords, we shall lie tonight together.

117. **sporting place:** playground.
122. **attach:** seize; see II. ii. 3.
126. **pawned:** pledged.
130. **due:** reward.
131. **Meet:** appropriate.
132. **shallowly:** thoughtlessly.
133. **Fondly:** foolishly.
134. **scattered stray:** dispersed stragglers.

[Re-]enter Westmoreland.

Now cousin, wherefore stands our army still?
   West. The leaders, having charge from you to 110
   stand,
Will not go off until they hear you speak.
   John. They know their duties.

[Re-]enter Hastings.

   Hast. My lord, our army is dispersed already.
Like youthful steers unyoked, they take their courses 115
East, west, north, south, or, like a school broke up,
Each hurries toward his home and sporting place.
   West. Good tidings, my Lord Hastings, for the
   which
I do arrest thee, traitor, of high treason. 120
And you, Lord Archbishop, and you, Lord Mowbray,
Of capital treason I attach you both.
   Mow. Is this proceeding just and honorable?
   West. Is your assembly so?
   Arch. Will you thus break your faith? 125
   John.   I pawned thee none.
I promised you redress of these same grievances
Whereof you did complain, which, by mine honor,
I will perform with a most Christian care.
But for you, rebels, look to taste the due 130
Meet for rebellion and such acts as yours.
Most shallowly did you these arms commence,
Fondly brought here and foolishly sent hence.
Strike up our drums, pursue the scattered stray.

IV. [iii.] Falstaff captures one Coleville of the Dale. Prince John is unimpressed and rebukes him for staying out of sight until the rebels had dispersed without a battle. He then orders his party to return to court because the King is seriously ill. Falstaff receives his permission to return through Gloucestershire (the home of Justice Shallow). Alone, he muses philosophically. He finds Prince John a dry bone in comparison with Hal and attributes his defects to the fact that he does not drink sherry.

<hr>

Ent. **excursions:** clashes of arms.

1. **condition:** rank.

6. **dale:** valley; hence, low, as is a dungeon.

12-3. **they are the drops of thy lovers:** i.e., my drops of sweat are like the tears of your friends; if I have to fight you, you will be killed.

15. **do observance:** show submission.

18-20. **I . . . name:** i.e., he is so well known for his fat belly that it immediately announces his identity.

God, and not we, hath safely fought today.   135
Some guard these traitors to the block of death,
Treason's true bed and yielder up of breath.

                                        [*Exeunt.*]

[Scene III. Another part of the Forest.]

Alarum; excursions. Enter *Falstaff* [and
            Coleville, meeting].

Fal. What's your name, sir? Of what condition are
you, and of what place, I pray?

Cole. I am a knight, sir, and my name is Coleville
of the Dale.

Fal. Well, then, Coleville is your name, a knight is   5
your degree, and your place the dale. Coleville shall
be still your name, a traitor your degree, and the
dungeon your place, a place deep enough. So shall
you be still Coleville of the dale.

Cole. Are not you Sir John Falstaff?   10

Fal. As good a man as he, sir, whoe'er I am. Do ye
yield, sir, or shall I sweat for you? If I do sweat, they
are the drops of thy lovers, and they weep for thy
death. Therefore rouse up fear and trembling, and
do observance to my mercy.   15

Cole. I think you are Sir John Falstaff, and in that
thought yield me.

Fal. I have a whole school of tongues in this belly
of mine, and not a tongue of them all speaks any

21. **indifferency:** inconsequential size.
22. **womb:** belly.
30-1. **but it should be thus:** if it were not thus (that I were thus taken to task).
34. **expedition:** speed.
36. **foundered:** lamed; **posts:** post horses.

other word but my name. An I had but a belly of   20
any indifferency, I were simply the most active fellow in Europe. My womb, my womb, my womb un-
does me. Here comes our general.

Enter *Prince John, Westmoreland,* [*Blunt,*]
and the rest. *Retreat* [*sounded*].

John. The heat is past, follow no further now.
Call in the powers, good cousin Westmoreland.   25
                    [*Exit Westmoreland.*]
Now, Falstaff, where have you been all this while?
When everything is ended, then you come.
These tardy tricks of yours will, on my life,
One time or other break some gallows' back.

Fal. I would be sorry, my lord, but it should be   30
thus. I never knew yet but rebuke and check was the
reward of valor. Do you think me a swallow, an
arrow, or a bullet? Have I, in my poor and old motion, the expedition of thought? I have speeded hither
with the very extremest inch of possibility. I have   35
foundered ninescore and odd posts, and here, travel-
tainted as I am, have, in my pure and immaculate
valor, taken Sir John Coleville of the Dale, a most
furious knight and valorous enemy. But what of that?
He saw me, and yielded, that I may justly say, with   40
the hook-nosed fellow of Rome, their Cæsar, "I came,
saw, and overcame."

John. It was more of his courtesy than your de-
serving.

Fal. I know not. Here he is, and here I yield him.   45

48. **particular ballad:** personal ballad; i.e., one specially printed to describe his valorous feats.

51. **gilt twopences:** i.e., silver coins gilded to give the appearance of solid gold; therefore, objects of less worth than they pretend.

53. **cinders of the element:** stars of the sky, which show as mere sparks of light.

67. **won them dearer than you have:** i.e., they would not have been taken without a fight.

72. **Retreat is made:** i.e., their troops have been called back.

And I beseech your Grace, let it be booked with the
rest of this day's deeds, or, by the Lord, I will have
it in a particular ballad else, with mine own picture
on the top on't, Coleville kissing my foot. To the
which course if I be enforced, if you do not all show   50
like gilt twopences to me, and I in the clear sky of
fame o'ershine you as much as the full moon doth
the cinders of the element, which show like pins'
heads to her, believe not the word of the noble.
Therefore let me have right, and let desert mount.   55

John. Thine's too heavy to mount.

Fal. Let it shine, then.

John. Thine's too thick to shine.

Fal. Let it do something, my good lord, that may
do me good, and call it what you will.   60

John. Is thy name Coleville?

Cole. It is, my lord.

John. A famous rebel art thou, Coleville.

Fal. And a famous true subject took him.

Cole. I am, my lord, but as my betters are   65
That led me hither. Had they been ruled by me,
You should have won them dearer than you have.

Fal. I know not how they sold themselves. But
thou, like a kind fellow, gavest thyself away gratis,
and I thank thee for thee.   70

Enter *Westmoreland.*

John. Now, have you left pursuit?

West. Retreat is made and execution stayed.

74. **present:** immediate.

77. **sore:** grievously; seriously.

80. **sober:** moderate.

84. **Stand . . . report:** be a good patron and report on me favorably.

85. **condition:** position.

92. **come to any proof:** prove themselves in trial; **thin drink:** small beer.

94. **greensickness:** a kind of anemia afflicting young girls near the age of puberty.

95. **get:** beget.

97. **inflammation:** excitement of the blood from drink.

99. **crudy:** curdled; clotted.

100. **apprehensive:** quick of understanding.

101. **forgetive:** presumably, capable of "forging" or creating; i.e., creative or imaginative; **fiery:** spirited.

John. Send Coleville with his confederates
To York, to present execution.
Blunt, lead him hence, and see you guard him sure.   75
        [*Exeunt Blunt and others with Coleville.*]
And now dispatch we toward the court, my lords.
I hear the King my father is sore sick.
Our news shall go before us to his Majesty,
Which, cousin, you shall bear to comfort him,
And we with sober speed will follow you.   80

Fal. My lord, I beseech you give me leave to go
Through Gloucestershire. And when you come to
        court,
Stand my good lord, pray, in your good report.

John. Fare you well, Falstaff. I, in my condition,   85
Shall better speak of you than you deserve.

                [*Exeunt all but Falstaff.*]

Fal. I would you had but the wit. 'Twere better
than your dukedom. Good faith, this same young
sober-blooded boy doth not love me, nor a man cannot make him laugh. But that's no marvel, he drinks 90
no wine. There's never none of these demure boys
come to any proof, for thin drink doth so overcool
their blood, and making many fish meals, that they
fall into a kind of male greensickness, and then, when
they marry, they get wenches. They are generally   95
fools and cowards, which some of us should be too,
but for inflammation. A good sherris sack hath a two-
fold operation in it. It ascends me into the brain;
dries me there all the foolish and dull and crudy
vapors which environ it; makes it apprehensive,   100
quick, forgetive, full of nimble, fiery, and delectable

106. **liver:** the source of courage in popular belief.

111-12. **vital commoners and inland petty spirits:** internal animal spirits; **muster me:** i.e., report for duty.

shapes, which, delivered o'er to the voice, the tongue,
which is the birth, becomes excellent wit. The second
property of your excellent sherris is the warming of
the blood, which, before cold and settled, left the   105
liver white and pale, which is the badge of pusillan-
imity and cowardice. But the sherris warms it and
makes it course from the inwards to the parts ex-
treme. It illumineth the face, which as a beacon gives
warning to all the rest of this little kingdom, man, to   110
arm, and then the vital commoners and inland petty
spirits muster me all to their captain, the heart, who,
great and puffed up with this retinue, doth any deed
of courage; and this valor comes of sherris. So that
skill in the weapon is nothing without sack, for that   115
sets it a-work; and learning a mere hoard of gold kept
by a devil, till sack commences it and sets it in act
and use. Hereof comes it that Prince Harry is valiant,
for the cold blood he did naturally inherit of his father, he hath, like lean, sterile, and bare land,   120
manured, husbanded, and tilled with excellent en-
deavor of drinking good and good store of fertile
sherris, that he is become very hot and valiant. If I
had a thousand sons, the first humane principle I
would teach them should be to forswear thin pota-   125
tions and to addict themselves to sack.

Enter *Bardolph.*

How now, Bardolph?
  Bar. The army is discharged all and gone.

130-32. **I . . . him:** I am already softening him up and soon can use him. The figure is that of melting wax to use with a seal.

||||||||||||||||||||||||||||||||||||||||||||||||||||||||||

IV. [**iv.**] The ailing King counsels his two younger sons to cultivate the companionship of Prince Hal but is pained to learn that the Prince is still in London with Poins and other disreputable friends. He fears for England under such a King unless the Prince alters his ways. Westmoreland arrives and reports the settlement of the rebellion. Word also comes that Northumberland and Lord Bardolph have met defeat in Yorkshire. Despite the good news the King is despondent; he faints away and has to be carried to a bed in another room.

||||||||||||||||||||||||||||||||||||||||||

5. **addressed:** prepared.
6. **Our substitutes in absence well invested:** i.e., the men who will act for me in my absence well established.
7. **lies level to:** accords with.

Fal. Let them go. I'll through Gloucestershire, and
there will I visit Master Robert Shallow, Esquire. I   130
have him already tempering between my finger and
my thumb, and shortly will I seal with him. Come
away.

[*Exeunt.*]

Scene [IV. Westminster. The Jerusalem Chamber.]

Enter the *King, Warwick, Thomas Duke of Clarence,
Humphrey of Gloucester,* [and *Others*].

King. Now, lords, if God doth give successful end
To this debate that bleedeth at our doors,
We will our youth lead on to higher fields
And draw no swords but what are sanctified.
Our navy is addressed, our power collected,   5
Our substitutes in absence well invested,
And everything lies level to our wish.
Only, we want a little personal strength,
And pause us, till these rebels, now afoot,
Come underneath the yoke of government.   10
War. Both which we doubt not but your Majesty
Shall soon enjoy.
King.   Humphrey, my son of Gloucester,
Where is the Prince your brother?
Glouc. I think he's gone to hunt, my lord, at   15
Windsor.

32. **omit:** neglect.

35. **observed:** shown dutiful attention; see **observance,** IV. [iii.] 15.

39. **humorous:** changeable.

40. **flaws:** dialect word for thin slivers of ice formed around the edge of water in winter.

43. **blood:** impulse.

46. **Confound:** destroy; **working:** violent agitation.

King. And how accompanied?
Glouc.   I do not know, my lord.
King. Is not his brother, Thomas of Clarence, with
    him?   20
Glouc. No, my good lord, he is in presence here.
Clar. What would my lord and father?
King. Nothing but well to thee, Thomas of Clar-
    ence.
How chance thou art not with the Prince thy brother?   25
He loves thee, and thou dost neglect him, Thomas;
Thou hast a better place in his affection
Than all thy brothers. Cherish it, my boy,
And noble offices thou mayst effect
Of mediation, after I am dead,   30
Between his greatness and thy other brethren.
Therefore omit him not, blunt not his love,
Nor lose the good advantage of his grace
By seeming cold or careless of his will.
For he is gracious, if he be observed.   35
He hath a tear for pity and a hand
Open as day for melting charity.
Yet notwithstanding, being incensed, he's flint,
As humorous as winter and as sudden
As flaws congealed in the spring of day.   40
His temper, therefore, must be well observed.
Chide him for faults, and do it reverently,
When you perceive his blood inclined to mirth;
But, being moody, give him time and scope,
Till that his passions, like a whale on ground,   45
Confound themselves with working. Learn this,
    Thomas,

51. **suggestion:** evil prompting; influence provoking dissension.

53. **work:** ferment.

54. **aconitum:** a deadly poison; **rash:** quick and violent of action.

61. **fattest:** most fertile.

67. **rotten:** morally corrupt.

71. **lavish:** unrestrained.

73. **fronting:** confronting in opposition.

74. **look beyond:** misunderstand.

And thou shalt prove a shelter to thy friends,
A hoop of gold to bind thy brothers in,
That the united vessel of their blood,   50
Mingled with venom of suggestion—
As, force perforce, the age will pour it in—
Shall never leak, though it do work as strong
As aconitum or rash gunpowder.
   Clar. I shall observe him with all care and love.   55
   King. Why art thou not at Windsor with him,
     Thomas?
   Clar. He is not there today; he dines in London.
   King. And how accompanied? Canst thou tell that?
   Clar. With Poins and other his continual followers.   60
   King. Most subject is the fattest soil to weeds,
And he, the noble image of my youth,
Is overspread with them. Therefore my grief
Stretches itself beyond the hour of death.
The blood weeps from my heart when I do shape   65
In forms imaginary the unguided days
And rotten times that you shall look upon
When I am sleeping with my ancestors.
For when his headstrong riot hath no curb,
When rage and hot blood are his counselors,   70
When means and lavish manners meet together,
O, with what wings shall his affections fly
Towards fronting peril and opposed decay!
   War. My gracious lord, you look beyond him
     quite.   75
The Prince but studies his companions
Like a strange tongue, wherein, to gain the language,

81. **terms:** words.

85. **mete:** evaluate.

100. **every course in his particular:** i.e., the details of the whole course of the action. **His** equals "its."

102. **haunch:** latter end.

'Tis needful that the most immodest word
Be looked upon and learned, which once attained,
Your Highness knows, comes to no further use   80
But to be known and hated. So, like gross terms,
The Prince will in the perfectness of time
Cast off his followers, and their memory
Shall as a pattern or a measure live,
By which his Grace must mete the lives of others,   85
Turning past evils to advantages.
    King. 'Tis seldom when the bee doth leave her
        comb
In the dead carrion.

Enter *Westmoreland.*

                    Who's here? Westmoreland?   90
    West. Health to my sovereign, and new happiness
Added to that that I am to deliver.
Prince John your son doth kiss your Grace's hand.
Mowbray, the Bishop Scroop, Hastings and all
Are brought to the correction of your law.   95
There is not now a rebel's sword unsheathed,
But Peace puts forth her olive everywhere.
The manner how this action hath been borne
Here at more leisure may your Highness read,
With every course in his particular.   100
    King. O Westmoreland, thou art a summer bird,
Which ever in the haunch of winter sings
The lifting up of day.

126-27. **look up:** take courage.

Enter *Harcourt*.

　　　　　Look, here's more news.

　Har. From enemies heaven keep your Majesty,　　105
And, when they stand against you, may they fall
As those that I am come to tell you of!
The Earl Northumberland and the Lord Bardolph,
With a great power of English and of Scots,
Are by the sheriff of Yorkshire overthrown.　　110
The manner and true order of the fight
This packet, please it you, contains at large.

　　King. And wherefore should these good news
　　　　make me sick?

Will Fortune never come with both hands full,　　115
But write her fair words still in foulest letters?
She either gives a stomach and no food—
Such are the poor, in health—or else a feast
And takes away the stomach—such are the rich,
That have abundance and enjoy it not.　　120
I should rejoice now at this happy news,
And now my sight fails, and my brain is giddy.
O me! Come near me. Now I am much ill.

　　Glouc. Comfort, your Majesty!

　　Clar.　　　　　　　　O my royal father!　125

　　West. My sovereign lord, cheer up yourself, look
　　　　up.

　War. Be patient, princes. You do know these fits
Are with his Highness very ordinary.
Stand from him, give him air, he'll straight be well.　130

　　Clar. No, no, he cannot long hold out these pangs.

133. **mure:** wall.

135. **fear me:** make me fearful.

136. **loathly:** loathsome; i.e., monstrously abnormal.

137. **as:** i.e., as if.

143. **Edward:** Edward III.

||||||||||||||||||||||||||||||||||||||||||||||||||

IV. [**v.**] Prince Henry comes in and is left alone with the sick King. Observing the crown on the pillow beside him, he attributes to it the responsibility for the King's illness. Thinking that his father's immobility means death, he places the crown on his own head and leaves the room. Warwick and the Prince's brothers return, and the King stirs to life. On learning that the Prince had been alone with him, he concludes bitterly that impatience for his death had caused his son to take away the crown. The Prince refutes this accusation with an eloquent statement of his love and the two are reconciled.

||||||||||||||||||||||||||||||||||||

3. **dull and favorable hand:** the hand of some obliging person playing softly.

The incessant care and labor of his mind
Hath wrought the mure that should confine it in
So thin that life looks through and will break out.
  Glouc. The people fear me, for they do observe   135
Unfathered heirs and loathly births of nature.
The seasons change their manners, as the year
Had found some months asleep and leaped them
    over.
  Clar. The river hath thrice flowed, no ebb between, 140
And the old folk, time's doting chronicles,
Say it did so a little time before
That our great-grandsire, Edward, sicked and died.
  War. Speak lower, princes, for the King recovers.
  Glouc. This apoplexy will certain be his end.   145
  King. I pray you, take me up, and bear me hence
Into some other chamber. Softly, pray.
              [Exeunt all, bearing the King.]

[Scene V. Another room in the palace.]

[The *King* lying on a bed; *Clarence, Gloucester,
    Warwick,* and *Others,* in attendance.]

  King. Let there be no noise made, my gentle
    friends,
Unless some dull and favorable hand
Will whisper music to my weary spirit.
  War. Call for the music in the other room.   5

19. **physic:** medicine.
28. **perturbation:** cause of distress.
29. **ports of slumber:** doors of sleep; i.e., eyes.
30. **watchful:** wakeful.
32. **biggin:** nightcap.

King. Set me the crown upon my pillow here.
Clar. His eye is hollow, and he changes much.
War. Less noise, less noise!

Enter *Prince Henry.*

Prince.   Who saw the Duke of Clarence?
Clar. I am here, brother, full of heaviness.   10
Prince. How now! Rain within doors, and none abroad!
How doth the King?
Glouc. Exceeding ill.
Prince.   Heard he the good news yet?   15
Tell it him.
Glouc. He altered much upon the hearing it.
Prince. If he be sick with joy, he'll recover without physic.
War. Not so much noise, my lords. Sweet Prince,   20
speak low.
The King your father is disposed to sleep.
Clar. Let us withdraw into the other room.
War. Will't please your Grace to go along with us?
Prince. No, I will sit and watch here by the King.   25
            [*Exeunt all but the Prince.*]
Why doth the crown lie there upon his pillow,
Being so troublesome a bedfellow?
O polished perturbation! Golden care!
That keepst the ports of slumber open wide
To many a watchful night! Sleep with it now!   30
Yet not so sound and half so deeply sweet
As he whose brow with homely biggin bound

36. **scaldst with safety:** burns the wearer at the same time as it protects him.

41. **rigol:** ring; i.e., the crown.

43. **heavy sorrows of the blood:** profound grief.

44. **nature:** natural feeling.

47-8. **as . . . me:** is inherited by me as the one closest to thee in blood and rank.

Snores out the watch of night. O majesty!
When thou dost pinch thy bearer, thou dost sit
Like a rich armor worn in heat of day,   35
That scaldst with safety. By his gates of breath
There lies a downy feather which stirs not.
Did he suspire, that light and weightless down
Perforce must move. My gracious lord! my father!
This sleep is sound indeed. This is a sleep   40
That from this golden rigol hath divorced
So many English kings. Thy due from me
Is tears and heavy sorrows of the blood,
Which nature, love, and filial tenderness
Shall, O dear father, pay thee plenteously.   45
My due from thee is this imperial crown,
Which, as immediate from thy place and blood,
Derives itself to me. [*Places crown on his head.*] Lo,
     where it sits,
Which God shall guard. And put the world's whole   50
     strength
Into one giant arm, it shall not force
This lineal honor from me. This from thee
Will I to mine leave, as 'tis left to me.   [*Exit.*]
     King. Warwick! Gloucester! Clarence!   55

Enter *Warwick, Gloucester, Clarence.*

     Clar. Doth the King call?
     War. What would your Majesty? How fares your
          Grace?
     King. Why did you leave me here alone, my lords?

76. **part:** act; **conjoins:** joins.

81. **thoughts:** worries.

84. **engrossed:** collected.

85. **cankered:** corroded; **strange-achieved:** ill-gotten.

86. **thoughtful:** heedful.

87. **arts:** skills.

88. **tolling:** taking toll; collecting.

89. **virtuous:** concentrated. The line is omitted from the Quarto.

Clar. We left the Prince my brother here, my liege,   60
Who undertook to sit and watch by you.
   King. The Prince of Wales! Where is he? Let me
     see him.
He is not here.
   War. This door is open; he is gone this way.   65
   Glouc. He came not through the chamber where
     we stayed.
   King. Where is the crown? Who took it from my
     pillow?
   War. When we withdrew, my liege, we left it here.   70
   King. The Prince hath ta'en it hence. Go, seek him
     out.
Is he so hasty that he doth suppose
My sleep my death?
Find him, my Lord of Warwick; chide him hither.   75
                        [*Exit Warwick.*]
This part of his conjoins with my disease
And helps to end me. See, sons, what things you are!
How quickly nature falls into revolt
When gold becomes her object!
For this the foolish overcareful fathers   80
Have broke their sleep with thoughts, their brains
     with care,
Their bones with industry.
For this they have engrossed and piled up
The cankered heaps of strange-achieved gold;   85
For this they have been thoughtful to invest
Their sons with arts and martial exercises.
When, like the bee, tolling from every flower
The virtuous sweets,

92-3. This . . . father: the dying father receives only this bitter taste from the wealth he has accumulated for his sons.

95. determined: ended.

98. With such a deep demeanor in great sorrow: showing such great sorrow.

106. Thy wish was father . . . to that thought: proverbial, dating at least from Cæsar's Gallic Commentaries, but most familiar in Shakespeare's phraseology.

112-13. my . . . wind: i.e., my continued life and function as King is sustained by such weak breathing.

Our thighs packed with wax, our mouths with honey,   90
We bring it to the hive, and, like the bees,
Are murdered for our pains. This bitter taste
Yields his engrossments to the ending father.

[Re-]enter *Warwick.*

Now, where is he that will not stay so long
Till his friend sickness hath determined me?   95
   War. My lord, I found the Prince in the next room,
Washing with kindly tears his gentle cheeks,
With such a deep demeanor in great sorrow
That tyranny, which never quaffed but blood,
Would, by beholding him, have washed his knife   100
With gentle eyedrops. He is coming hither.
   King. But wherefore did he take away the crown?

Enter *Prince Henry.*

Lo, where he comes. Come hither to me, Harry.
Depart the chamber, leave us here alone.
                    Exeunt [*Warwick and the rest*].
   Prince. I never thought to hear you speak again.   105
   King. Thy wish was father, Harry, to that thought.
I stay too long by thee, I weary thee.
Dost thou so hunger for mine empty chair
That thou wilt needs invest thee with my honors
Before thy hour be ripe? O foolish youth!   110
Thou seekst the greatness that will overwhelm thee.
Stay but a little, for my cloud of dignity
Is held from falling with so weak a wind

117. **sealed up:** confirmed.

123. **forbear:** tolerate.

128. **balm:** anointing oil, such as was used in coronation ceremonies.

129. **compound:** combine.

132. **form:** ceremony.

133. **vanity:** foolishness.

136. **apes of idleness:** frivolous fools.

That it will quickly drop. My day is dim.
Thou hast stolen that which after some few hours   115
Were thine without offense; and at my death
Thou hast sealed up my expectation.
Thy life did manifest thou lovedst me not,
And thou wilt have me die assured of it.
Thou hidest a thousand daggers in thy thoughts,   120
Which thou hast whetted on thy stony heart,
To stab at half an hour of my life.
What! Canst thou not forbear me half an hour?
Then get thee gone and dig my grave thyself,
And bid the merry bells ring to thine ear   125
That thou art crowned, not that I am dead.
Let all the tears that should bedew my hearse
Be drops of balm to sanctify thy head.
Only compound me with forgotten dust;
Give that which gave thee life unto the worms.   130
Pluck down my officers, break my decrees,
For now a time is come to mock at form.
Harry the Fifth is crowned. Up, vanity!
Down, royal state! All you sage counselors, hence!
And to the English court assemble now,   135
From every region, apes of idleness!
Now, neighbor confines, purge you of your scum.
Have you a ruffian that will swear, drink, dance,
Revel the night, rob, murder, and commit
The oldest sins the newest kind of ways?   140
Be happy, he will trouble you no more.
England shall double gild his treble guilt,
England shall give him office, honor, might,
For the fifth Harry from curbed license plucks

146. **flesh his tooth on:** taste the flesh of.

147. **civil:** domestic.

154. **dear and deep:** severe.

158. **affect:** aspire to.

160. **obedience:** bow of homage.

172. **depending:** hanging; i.e., being connected to thee.

The muzzle of restraint, and the wild dog   145
Shall flesh his tooth on every innocent.
O my poor kingdom, sick with civil blows!
When that my care could not withhold thy riots,
What wilt thou do when riot is thy care?
O, thou wilt be a wilderness again,   150
Peopled with wolves, thy old inhabitants.
   Prince. O, pardon me, my liege! But for my tears,
The moist impediments unto my speech,
I had forestalled this dear and deep rebuke
Ere you with grief had spoke and I had heard   155
The course of it so far. There is your crown,
And He that wears the crown immortally
Long guard it yours. If I affect it more
Than as your honor and as your renown,
Let me no more from this obedience rise,   160
Which my most inward true and duteous spirit
Teacheth, this prostrate and exterior bending.
God witness with me, when I here came in,
And found no course of breath within your Majesty,
How cold it struck my heart. If I do feign,   165
O let me in my present wildness die
And never live to show the incredulous world
The noble change that I have purposed.
Coming to look on you, thinking you dead,
And dead almost, my liege, to think you were,   170
I spake unto this crown as having sense,
And thus upbraided it: "The care on thee depending
Hath fed upon the body of my father.
Therefore, thou best of gold art worst of gold.
Other, less fine in carat, is more precious,   175

176. **medicine:** gold was believed to have medicinal virtues; **potable:** drinkable.

184. **strain:** element.

186. **affection of:** inclination toward; see II. iii. 30.

196. **latest:** last.

198. **indirect crooked:** devious, dishonest.

202. **opinion:** credit.

205. **boisterous:** violent.

Making "medicine potable" from gold.

From Konrad Gesner, *The Practice of the New and Old Physic* (1599).

Preserving life in medicine potable;
But thou, most fine, most honored, most renowned,
Hast eat thy bearer up." Thus, my most royal liege,
Accusing it, I put it on my head,
To try with it, as with an enemy   180
That had before my face murdered my father,
The quarrel of a true inheritor.
But if it did infect my blood with joy,
Or swell my thoughts to any strain of pride,
If any rebel or vain spirit of mine   185
Did with the least affection of a welcome
Give entertainment to the might of it,
Let God forever keep it from my head
And make me as the poorest vassal is
That doth with awe and terror kneel to it.   190
  King. O my son,
God put it in thy mind to take it hence,
That thou mightst win the more thy father's love,
Pleading so wisely in excuse of it!
Come hither, Harry, sit thou by my bed,   195
And hear, I think, the very latest counsel
That ever I shall breathe. God knows, my son,
By what bypaths and indirect crooked ways
I met this crown, and I myself know well
How troublesome it sat upon my head.   200
To thee it shall descend with better quiet,
Better opinion, better confirmation,
For all the soil of the achievement goes
With me into the earth. It seemed in me
But as an honor snatched with boisterous hand,   205
And I had many living to upbraid

209. **bold fears:** great hazards.

210. **answered:** encountered by fighting.

212. **argument:** subject.

213. **purchased:** gained as the spoils of war.

215. **garland:** crown; **successively:** by right of succession.

217. **griefs are green:** grievances are new.

221. **fell:** ruthless.

222. **lodge:** entertain.

228. **giddy:** inconstant; unreliable.

229. **hence borne out:** carried out in foreign parts.

230. **waste:** destroy; see I. [iii.] 66.

231. **would I:** i.e., would I say.

My gain of it by their assistances,
Which daily grew to quarrel and to bloodshed
Wounding supposed peace. All these bold fears
Thou seest with peril I have answered,   210
For all my reign hath been but as a scene
Acting that argument. And now my death
Changes the mode, for what in me was purchased
Falls upon thee in a more fairer sort,
So thou the garland wearst successively.   215
Yet, though thou standst more sure than I could do,
Thou art not firm enough, since griefs are green.
And all my friends, which thou must make thy
    friends,
Have but their stings and teeth newly ta'en out,   220
By whose fell working I was first advanced
And by whose power I well might lodge a fear
To be again displaced. Which to avoid,
I cut them off, and had a purpose now
To lead out many to the Holy Land,   225
Lest rest and lying still might make them look
Too near unto my state. Therefore, my Harry,
Be it thy course to busy giddy minds
With foreign quarrels, that action, hence borne out,
May waste the memory of the former days.   230
More would I, but my lungs are wasted so
That strength of speech is utterly denied me.
How I came by the crown, O God forgive,
And grant it may with thee in true peace live!
    Prince. My gracious liege,   235
You won it, wore it, kept it, gave it me.
Then plain and right must my possession be,

247. **thy sight:** the sight of thee.
248. **period:** conclusion.

Which I with more than with a common pain
'Gainst all the world will rightfully maintain.

Enter *Lord John of Lancaster* and *Warwick.*

King. Look, look, here comes my John of Lan-   240
caster.
John. Health, peace, and happiness to my royal
father!
King. Thou bringst me happiness and peace, son
John,   245
But health, alack, with youthful wings is flown
From this bare withered trunk. Upon thy sight
My worldly business makes a period.
Where is my Lord of Warwick?
Prince.   My Lord of Warwick!   250
King. Doth any name particular belong
Unto the lodging where I first did swoon?
War. 'Tis called Jerusalem, my noble lord.
King. Laud be to God! Even there my life must
end.   255
It hath been prophesied to me many years
I should not die but in Jerusalem,
Which vainly I supposed the Holy Land.
But bear me to that chamber; there I'll lie.
In that Jerusalem shall Harry die.   260

[*Exeunt.*]

THE HISTORY OF
HENRY
THE FOURTH
[PART 2]

ACT V

V. i. Falstaff receives a warm welcome from Justice Shallow, who invites him to stay the night. The old rogue sees in the foolish justice limitless possibilities for gulling, and looks forward to reporting the comedy to the Prince.

⠀⠀⠀⠀⠀⠀⠀‖‖‖‖‖‖‖‖‖‖‖‖‖‖‖‖‖‖‖‖‖‖‖‖‖‖‖

1. **By cock and pie:** an oath of imprecise meaning, though **cock** is a corruption of God.

13. **precepts:** writs.

14. **headland:** section of unplowed land left to mark the boundary between two farmers' holdings.

ACT V

Scene I. [Gloucestershire. Shallow's house.]

Enter *Shallow, Falstaff,* and *Bardolph* [and *Page*].

Shal. By cock and pie, sir, you shall not away tonight. What, Davy, I say!

Fal. You must excuse me, Master Robert Shallow.

Shal. I will not excuse you; you shall not be excused; excuses shall not be admitted; there is no excuse shall serve; you shall not be excused. Why, Davy! 5

[Enter *Davy*.]

Davy. Here, sir.

Shal. Davy, Davy, Davy, Davy; let me see, Davy. Let me see, Davy, let me see. Yea, marry, William 10 cook, bid him come hither. Sir John, you shall not be excused.

Davy. Marry, sir, thus: those precepts cannot be served. And, again, sir, shall we sow the headland with wheat? 15

16. **red wheat:** winter wheat.

18. **note:** account.

20. **cast:** summed up.

26. **answer:** pay for.

28. **kickshaws:** dainties; a corruption of the French *quelque chose* (something).

32. **arrant:** out-and-out; see II. i. 38.

36. **Well conceited:** well conceived; a clever quip.

38. **countenance:** favor; see IV. i. 41. and IV. [ii.] 14.

Shal. With red wheat, Davy. But for William
cook—are there no young pigeons?

Davy. Yes, sir. Here is now the smith's note for
shoeing and plow-irons.

Shal. Let it be cast and paid. Sir John, you shall   20
not be excused.

Davy. Now, sir, a new link to the bucket must
needs be had. And, sir, do you mean to stop any of
William's wages, about the sack he lost the other day
at Hinckley fair?   25

Shal. 'A shall answer it. Some pigeons, Davy, a
couple of short-legged hens, a joint of mutton, and
any pretty little tiny kickshaws, tell William cook.

Davy. Doth the man of war stay all night, sir?

Shal. Yea, Davy. I will use him well. A friend i'   30
the court is better than a penny in purse. Use his men
well, Davy, for they are arrant knaves and will back-
bite.

Davy. No worse than they are backbitten, sir, for
they have marvelous foul linen.   35

Shal. Well conceited, Davy. About thy business,
Davy.

Davy. I beseech you, sir, to countenance William
Visor of Woncot against Clement Perkes o' the hill.

Shal. There is many complaints, Davy, against that   40
Visor. That Visor is an arrant knave, on my knowledge.

Davy. I grant your worship that he is a knave, sir,
but yet, God forbid, sir, but a knave should have
some countenance at his friend's request. An honest   45
man, sir, is able to speak for himself, when a knave is

48-9. **bear out:** back up.

53-4. **Look about:** be alert; get on with your duties.

63. **quantities:** fragments.

66. **semblable coherence:** resemblance.

70-1. **married in conjunction with the participation of society:** closely joined because of long association with each other; **consent:** accord.

74. **near:** intimate with; **curry with:** curry favor with; butter up.

76, 77. **bearing, carriage:** behavior.

not. I have served your worship truly, sir, this eight
years, and if I cannot once or twice in a quarter bear
out a knave against an honest man, I have but a very
little credit with your worship. The knave is mine   50
honest friend, sir. Therefore, I beseech you, let him
be countenanced.

Shal. Go to, I say he shall have no wrong. Look
about, Davy. [*Exit Davy.*] Where are you, Sir John?
Come, come, come, off with your boots. Give me your   55
hand, Master Bardolph.

Bard. I am glad to see your worship.

Shal. I thank thee with all my heart, kind Master
Bardolph. [*To the Page*] And welcome, my tall fellow. Come, Sir John.   60

Fal. I'll follow you, good Master Robert Shallow.
[*Exit Shallow.*] Bardolph, look to our horses. [*Exeunt
Bardolph and Page.*] If I were sawed into quantities,
I should make four dozen of such bearded hermits'
staves as Master Shallow. It is a wonderful thing to   65
see the semblable coherence of his men's spirits and
his. They, by observing him, do bear themselves like
foolish justices; he, by conversing with them, is
turned into a justice-like servingman. Their spirits are
so married in conjunction with the participation of   70
society that they flock together in consent, like so
many wild geese. If I had a suit to Master Shallow,
I would humor his men with the imputation of being
near their master; if to his men, I would curry with
Master Shallow that no man could better command   75
his servants. It is certain that either wise bearing or
ignorant carriage is caught, as men take diseases, one

81. **four terms:** a year, comprising the four legal terms Michaelmas, Hilary, Easter, and Trinity.

82. **actions:** legal actions, as in II. i. 1; **intervallums:** intervals.

84-5. **a fellow that never had the ache in his shoulders:** i.e., a young man such as Prince Hal, who has never done a day's work.

86. **ill laid up:** carelessly stored, hence, wrinkled.

\==

V. ii. News of the King's death makes his officials apprehensive of the changes that may come with the accession of his unruly oldest son, Prince Henry. But the Prince reassures them all that he will show himself a Christian king. In particular, he declares his respect for the Lord Chief Justice, who had expected reprisal for having sent the Prince to prison, and he admonishes the old man to continue dispensing true justice.

of another. Therefore let men take heed of their company. I will devise matter enough out of this Shallow
to keep Prince Harry in continual laughter the wear-   80
ing out of six fashions, which is four terms, or two
actions; and 'a shall laugh without intervallums. O, it
is much that a lie with a slight oath and a jest with a
sad brow will do with a fellow that never had the
ache in his shoulders! O, you shall see him laugh till   85
his face be like a wet cloak ill laid up!

Shal. [*Within*] Sir John!

Fal. I come, Master Shallow, I come, Master Shallow.

[*Exit.*]

Scene II. [Westminster. The palace.]

Enter *Warwick* and the *Lord Chief Justice*.

War. How now, my Lord Chief Justice! whither
  away?
Just. How doth the King?
War. Exceeding well. His cares are now all ended.
Just. I hope, not dead.   5
War.   He's walked the way of nature,
And to our purposes he lives no more.
Just. I would his Majesty had called me with him.
The service that I truly did his life
Hath left me open to all injuries.   10

15. **fantasy:** fancy.

16. **heavy:** sorrowful; as at I. [i.] 137; **issue:** children.

20. **strike sail:** salute; show submission to.

Prince Hal as King Henry V.

From Hubert Goltzius, *Antiquissima nobilissimaque Anglorum regum* (1586).

War. Indeed I think the young King loves you not.
Just. I know he doth not, and do arm myself
To welcome the condition of the time,
Which cannot look more hideously upon me
Than I have drawn it in my fantasy.   15

Enter *John of Lancaster, Thomas* [*of Clarence*], and
     Humphrey [*of Gloucester, Westmoreland, and*
                        Others].

War. Here come the heavy issue of dead Harry.
O that the living Harry had the temper
Of him, the worst of these three gentlemen!
How many nobles then should hold their places
That must strike sail to spirits of vile sort!   20
Just. O God, I fear all will be overturned!
John. Good morrow, cousin Warwick, good mor-
     row.
Glouc.⎫
Clar. ⎬ Good morrow, cousin.
John. We meet like men that had forgot to speak. 25
War. We do remember, but our argument
Is all too heavy to admit much talk.
John. Well, peace be with him that hath made us
     heavy.
Just. Peace be with us, lest we be heavier.   30
Glouc. O good my lord, you have lost a friend
     indeed,
And I dare swear you borrow not that face
Of seeming sorrow, it is sure your own.

35. **grace:** favor (from the new King).

41. **swims against your stream of quality:** i.e., is contrary to your high estate.

44-5. **beg/A ragged and forestalled remission:** beg in a contemptible fashion for a pardon that is certain to be denied.

55. **Amurath:** a Turkish sultan who had become a byword for tyranny because he ordered his brothers slaughtered when he came to the throne.

59. **deeply:** with deep seriousness.

John. Though no man be assured what grace to   35
    find,
You stand in coldest expectation.
I am the sorrier; would 'twere otherwise.
   Clar. Well, you must now speak Sir John Falstaff
    fair,   40
Which swims against your stream of quality.
   Just. Sweet princes, what I did, I did in honor,
Led by the impartial conduct of my soul,
And never shall you see that I will beg
A ragged and forestalled remission.   45
If truth and upright innocency fail me,
I'll to the King my master that is dead,
And tell him who hath sent me after him.
   War. Here comes the Prince.

Enter the *Prince* [as *King Henry the Fifth*] and
               Blunt.

   Just. Good morrow, and God save your Majesty!   50
   Prince. This new and gorgeous garment, majesty,
Sits not so easy on me as you think.
Brothers, you mix your sadness with some fear.
This is the English, not the Turkish court;
Not Amurath an Amurath succeeds,   55
But Harry Harry. Yet be sad, good brothers,
For, by my faith, it very well becomes you.
Sorrow so royally in you appears
That I will deeply put the fashion on
And wear it in my heart. Why then, be sad,   60
But entertain no more of it, good brothers,
Than a joint burden laid upon us all.

70. **strangely:** i.e., with hostility.

79. **easy:** slight, of no importance.

80. **Lethe:** a river in Hades that produced forgetfulness in those who drank its waters. Shakespeare uses the term ambiguously.

81. **use the person:** i.e., assume the function.

For me, by heaven, I bid you be assured,
I'll be your father and your brother too.
Let me but bear your love, I'll bear your cares.   65
Yet weep that Harry's dead, and so will I;
But Harry lives, that shall convert those tears
By number into hours of happiness.
 Brothers. We hope no other from your Majesty.
 Prince. You all look strangely on me.   70
[*To the Chief Justice*] And you most.
You are, I think, assured I love you not.
 Just. I am assured, if I be measured rightly,
Your Majesty hath no just cause to hate me.
 Prince. No?   75
How might a prince of my great hopes forget
So great indignities you laid upon me?
What! Rate, rebuke, and roughly send to prison
The immediate heir of England! Was this easy?
May this be washed in Lethe, and forgotten?   80
 Just. I then did use the person of your father;
The image of his power lay then in me.
And, in the administration of his law,
Whiles I was busy for the commonwealth,
Your Highness pleased to forget my place,   85
The majesty and power of law and justice,
The image of the King whom I presented,
And struck me in my very seat of judgment;
Whereon, as an offender to your father,
I gave bold way to my authority   90
And did commit you. If the deed were ill,
Be you contented, wearing now the garland,
To have a son set your decrees at nought,

94. **awful:** awe-inspiring.

97. **spurn at:** show contempt for.

98. **your workings in a second body:** the deputy who acts for you.

99. **Question your royal thoughts, make the case yours:** i.e., look at the circumstances as though you had been the King.

100. **propose:** imagine.

105. **soft silencing:** gently restraining.

106. **cold considerance:** cool reflection.

107. **in your state:** i.e., as a king.

118. **proper:** very own.

124. **remembrance:** reminder.

To pluck down justice from your awful bench,
To trip the course of law and blunt the sword   95
That guards the peace and safety of your person;
Nay, more, to spurn at your most royal image
And mock your workings in a second body.
Question your royal thoughts, make the case yours;
Be now the father and propose a son;   100
Hear your own dignity so much profaned;
See your most dreadful laws so loosely slighted;
Behold yourself so by a son disdained;
And then imagine me taking your part
And in your power soft silencing your son.   105
After this cold considerance, sentence me,
And, as you are a king, speak in your state
What I have done that misbecame my place,
My person, or my liege's sovereignty.

  Prince. You are right, Justice, and you weigh this 110
    well.
Therefore still bear the balance and the sword;
And I do wish your honors may increase,
Till you do live to see a son of mine
Offend you and obey you, as I did.   115
So shall I live to speak my father's words:
"Happy am I, that have a man so bold
That dares do justice on my proper son,
And not less happy, having such a son
That would deliver up his greatness so   120
Into the hands of justice." You did commit me.
For which, I do commit into your hand
The unstained sword that you have used to bear,
With this remembrance, that you use the same

133. **my affections:** i.e., all the wild impulses that I formerly displayed; see **affection,** II. iii. 30 and IV. [v.] 186.

137. **Rotten:** unsound; see IV. i. 172.

138-39. **The tide of blood in me/Hath proudly flowed in vanity till now:** I have allowed my foolishness to run rampant until now.

141. **mingle with the state of floods:** blend with the majestic ocean.

150. **accite:** call; see II. ii. 59.

151. **remembered:** mentioned; **all our state:** i.e., the High Court of Parliament referred to in l. 143.

152. **consigning:** subscribing; that is, if God supports my good intentions.

With the like bold, just, and impartial spirit   125
As you have done 'gainst me. There is my hand.
You shall be as a father to my youth.
My voice shall sound as you do prompt mine ear,
And I will stoop and humble my intents
To your well-practiced wise directions.   130
And, princes all, believe me, I beseech you,
My father is gone wild into his grave,
For in his tomb lie my affections,
And with his spirit sadly I survive,
To mock the expectation of the world,   135
To frustrate prophecies and to raze out
Rotten opinion, who hath writ me down
After my seeming. The tide of blood in me
Hath proudly flowed in vanity till now.
Now doth it turn and ebb back to the sea,   140
Where it shall mingle with the state of floods
And flow henceforth in formal majesty.
Now call we our High Court of Parliament.
And let us choose such limbs of noble counsel
That the great body of our state may go   145
In equal rank with the best-governed nation;
That war, or peace, or both at once, may be
As things acquainted and familiar to us,
In which you, father, shall have foremost hand.
Our coronation done, we will accite,   150
As I before remembered, all our state.
And, God consigning to my good intents,
No prince nor peer shall have just cause to say,
God shorten Harry's happy life one day!

Exeunt.

V. iii. Falstaff, still with Shallow, is informed by Pistol that Prince Hal is now the King. In great excitement, Falstaff decides to set out at once for London, where he feels certain of favor and preferment.

iiiiiiiiiiiiiiiiiiiiiiiiiiiiiiiiiiiiiii

2. **pippin:** apple.

3. **graffing:** grafting; **caraways:** a confection containing caraway seeds.

8. **Spread:** set the table.

11. **husband:** household manager.

12. **varlet:** menial.

16. **quoth-a:** said he; i.e., as the author of the song said.

22. **ever among:** all the while.

Scene III. [Gloucestershire. Shallow's orchard.]

Enter *Sir John Falstaff, Shallow, Silence, Davy,*
Bardolph, Page.

Shal. Nay, you shall see my orchard, where, in an
arbor, we will eat a last year's pippin of my own
graffing, with a dish of caraways, and so forth. Come,
cousin Silence. And then to bed.

Fal. 'Fore God, you have here a goodly dwelling   5
and a rich.

Shal. Barren, barren, barren. Beggars all, beggars
all, Sir John. Marry, good air. Spread, Davy; spread,
Davy. Well said, Davy.

Fal. This Davy serves you for good uses. He is your   10
servingman and your husband.

Shal. A good varlet, a good varlet, a very good varlet, Sir John. By the mass, I have drunk too much
sack at supper. A good varlet. Now sit down, now sit
down. Come, cousin.   15

Sil. Ah, sirrah! quoth-a, we shall

[*Sings*] Do nothing but eat, and make good cheer,
    And praise God for the merry year,
    When flesh is cheap and females dear,
    And lusty lads roam here and there   20
        So merrily,
    And ever among so merrily.

Fal. There's a merry heart! Good Master Silence,
I'll give you a health for that anon.

Shal. Give Master Bardolph some wine, Davy.   25

28. **Proface:** perhaps from the obsolete French phrase *bon prou vous fasse;* the meaning is roughly equivalent to "good cheer"; **want in meat:** lack in food.

29. **you must bear, the heart's all:** you must be tolerant, a cheerful heart is the main thing.

36. **Shrovetide:** the three days before Ash Wednesday. Shrove Tuesday was a particular time of merrymaking.

39. **mettle:** spirit, see I. [i.] 132.

42-3. **leathercoats:** russet apples, which have leathery skins.

47. **brisk and fine:** tangy and clear.

48. **the leman mine:** my sweetheart.

Davy. Sweet sir, sit, I'll be with you anon. Most
sweet sir, sit. Master page, good master page, sit.
Proface! What you want in meat, we'll have in drink.
But you must bear, the heart's all.   [*Exit.*]

Shal. Be merry, Master Bardolph, and, my little   30
soldier there, be merry.

Sil. [*Sings*] Be merry, be merry, my wife has all,
          For women are shrews, both short and
               tall.
          'Tis merry in hall when beards wag all,   35
               And welcome merry Shrovetide.
          Be merry, be merry.

Fal. I did not think Master Silence had been a man
of this mettle.

Sil. Who, I? I have been merry twice and once ere   40
now.

[Re-]enter *Davy.*

Davy. [*To Bardolph*] There's a dish of leathercoats for you.

Shal. Davy!

Davy. Your worship! [*To Bardolph*] I'll be with   45
you straight.—A cup of wine, sir?

Sil. [*Sings*] A cup of wine that's brisk and fine,
          And drink unto the leman mine,
          And a merry heart lives long-a.

Fal. Well said, Master Silence.   50

Sil. An we shall be merry, now comes in the sweet
o' the night.

61. **cabileros:** cavaliers; gallants.

66. **pottle-pot:** two-quart container; see II. ii. 78.

67. **liggens:** a dialect word meaning "capacity." The oath has not been noted elsewhere.

69. **out:** pass out.

74. **done me right:** matched me drink for drink; "done me proud."

75-7. **Do . . . Samingo:** apparently a parody of a song in Thomas Nashe's *Summer's Last Will and Testament* (1592): "God Bacchus doe him right and dub him knight, Domingo."

Fal. Health and long life to you, Master Silence.

Sil. [*Sings*] Fill the cup, and let it come,
               I'll pledge you a mile to the   55
                    bottom.

Shal. Honest Bardolph, welcome. If thou wantst
anything, and wilt not call, beshrew thy heart. [*To
the Page*] Welcome, my little tiny thief, and welcome
indeed too. I'll drink to Master Bardolph, and to all   60
the cabileros about London.

Davy. I hope to see London once ere I die.

Bar. An I might see you there, Davy—

Shal. By the mass, you'll crack a quart together, ha!
Will you not, Master Bardolph?   65

Bar. Yea, sir, in a pottle-pot.

Shal. By God's liggens, I thank thee. The knave
will stick by thee, I can assure thee that. 'A will not
out, he is true bred.

Bar. And I'll stick by him, sir. *One knocks at door.*   70

Shal. Why, there spoke a king. Lack nothing. Be
merry. Look who's at door there, ho! Who knocks?
                                        [*Exit Davy.*]

Fal. [*To Silence, who has drunk up*] Why, now
you have done me right.

Sil. [*Sings*] Do me right,   75
               And dub me knight.
                    Samingo.

Is't not so?

Fal. 'Tis so.

Sil. Is't so? Why then, say an old man can do some-   80
what.

91. **but:** except for; **goodman:** a title usually given a yeoman; i.e., one who has at least a small holding of land.

94. **recreant:** cowardly (one who breaks faith).

99-100. **like a man of this world:** i.e., in plain English.

101. **foutra:** an indecent word.

103-4. **O . . . thereof:** Falstaff falls into Pistol's ranting cadences; **King Cophetua:** the hero of a ballad who married a beggar maid. Falstaff probably uses the name only because of its ring.

106. **Helicons:** Muses, because Mount Helicon was their home.

107. **baffled:** treated with contempt.

108. **Furies:** the avenging female deities of classical legend.

[Re-]enter *Davy*.

Davy. An't please your worship, there's one Pistol
come from the court with news.

Fal. From the court! Let him come in.

Enter *Pistol*.

How now, Pistol!   85

Pist. Sir John, God save you!

Fal. What wind blew you hither, Pistol?

Pist. Not the ill wind which blows no man to good.
Sweet knight, thou art now one of the greatest men in
this realm.   90

Sil. By'r lady, I think 'a be, but goodman Puff of
Barson.

Pist. Puff!
Puff i' thy teeth, most recreant coward base!
Sir John, I am thy Pistol and thy friend,   95
And helter-skelter have I rode to thee,
And tidings do I bring, and lucky joys,
And golden times, and happy news of price.

Fal. I pray thee now, deliver them like a man of
this world.   100

Pist. A foutra for the world and worldlings base!
I speak of Africa and golden joys.

Fal. O base Assyrian knight, what is thy news?
Let King Cophetua know the truth thereof.

Sil. [*Sings*] And Robin Hood, Scarlet, and John.   105

Pist. Shall dunghill curs confront the Helicons?
And shall good news be baffled?
Then, Pistol, lay thy head in Furies' lap.

115. **Besonian:** base scoundrel, probably from the Italian *bisogno*, needy fellow.

122. **do this, and fig me:** an indecent gesture with the thumb and forefinger, sometimes known as "the fig of Spain."

125. **just:** true.

Shal. Honest gentleman, I know not your breeding.

Pist. Why then, lament therefore.   110

Shal. Give me pardon, sir. If, sir, you come with
news from the court, I take it there's but two ways:
either to utter them, or to conceal them. I am, sir,
under the King, in some authority.

Pist. Under which King, Besonian? Speak, or die. 115

Shal. Under King Harry.

Pist.   Harry the Fourth? or Fifth?

Shal. Harry the Fourth.

Pist.   A foutra for thine office!
Sir John, thy tender lambkin now is King.   120
Harry the Fifth's the man. I speak the truth.
When Pistol lies, do this, and fig me, like
The bragging Spaniard.

Fal. What, is the old King dead?

Pist. As nail in door. The things I speak are just. 125

Fal. Away, Bardolph! Saddle my horse. Master
Robert Shallow, choose what office thou wilt in the
land, 'tis thine. Pistol, I will double charge thee with
dignities.

Bard. O joyful day!   130
I would not take a knighthood for my fortune.

Pist. What! I do bring good news.

Fal. Carry Master Silence to bed. Master Shallow,
my Lord Shallow—be what thou wilt, I am fortune's
steward—get on thy boots. We'll ride all night. O 135
sweet Pistol! Away, Bardolph! [*Exit Bardolph.*]
Come, Pistol, utter more to me, and withal devise
something to do thyself good. Boot, boot, Master
Shallow. I know the young King is sick for me. Let us

144. **Where is the life that late I led:** a phrase from a ballad, also quoted in *The Taming of the Shrew,* IV. i. 143.

||||||||||||||||||||||||||||||||||||||||||||||||||||||||

V. iv. As an indication of the new spirit abroad, officers carry Quickly and Doll Tearsheet off to prison.

||||||||||||||||||||||||||||||||||||||||||

5. **whipping cheer:** whipping as her cheer (fare or diet).

8. **Nuthook:** a hooked stick for pulling down limbs of a nut tree, probably applied to the officer because he carried a weapon which looked like a **nuthook.**

9. **tripe-visaged:** ugly-faced.

11. **paper-faced:** white and thin of face.

16. **a dozen of cushions:** Doll has borrowed a cushion from the Hostess to make herself look pregnant. Whores frequently pretended pregnancy to escape corporal punishment.

take any man's horses; the laws of England are at my 140
commandment. Blessed are they that have been my
friends, and woe to my Lord Chief Justice!

    Pist. Let vultures vile seize on his lungs also!
"Where is the life that late I led?" say they.
Why, here it is. Welcome these pleasant days! 145

                              Exeunt.

Scene IV. [London. A street.]

Enter *Hostess Quickly, Doll Tearsheet,* and *Beadles.*

    Host. No, thou arrant knave, I would to God that I
might die, that I might have thee hanged. Thou hast
drawn my shoulder out of joint.

    Beadle. The constables have delivered her over to
me, and she shall have whipping cheer enough, I 5
warrant her. There hath been a man or two lately
killed about her.

    Doll. Nuthook, nuthook, you lie. Come on, I'll tell
thee what, thou damned tripe-visaged rascal, an the
child I now go with do miscarry, thou wert better 10
thou hadst struck thy mother, thou paper-faced
villain.

    Host. O the Lord, that Sir John were come! He
would make this a bloody day to somebody. But I
pray God the fruit of her womb miscarry! 15

    Beadle. If it do, you shall have a dozen of cushions

19. **amongst:** between.

20. **thin man in a censer:** another gibe at the beadle's extraordinary thinness. A **censer** is a container in which to burn incense.

21-22. **swinged:** beaten; **bluebottle:** i.e., blue-clad. Beadles, like modern policemen, wore blue uniforms.

23. **half-kirtles:** skirts.

27. **of sufferance comes ease:** proverbial. **Sufferance** equals suffering.

32. **atomy:** anatomy; i.e., skeleton.

33. **rascal:** used in the sense of "lean deer," as at II. iv. 41.

ıı

V. v. Falstaff, Shallow, Pistol, and Bardolph wait for the King to pass through the streets of London. When Henry V appears, Falstaff and Pistol greet him familiarly, but the King spurns Falstaff and orders the Lord Chief Justice to see to his banishment on pain of death. Falstaff assures his friends that the King will call for him in secret, but the Lord Chief Justice and Prince John order officers to carry them all off to Fleet Prison.

The King has summoned Parliament and Prince John prophesies that before the year is over an expedition to France will be on its way.

ıııııııııııııııııııııııııııııııııı

Ent. rushes: usually spread on floors instead of rugs or carpets, **rushes** were also strewn on the streets for festive occasions, particularly in advance of a royal procession.

again. You have but eleven now. Come, I charge you
both go with me, for the man is dead that you and
Pistol beat amongst you.

Doll. I'll tell you what, you thin man in a censer, I   20
will have you as soundly swinged for this. You bluebottle rogue, you filthy famished correctioner, if you
be not swinged, I'll forswear half-kirtles.

Beadle. Come, come, you she knight-errant,
come.   25

Host. O God, that right should thus overcome
might! Well, of sufferance comes ease.

Doll. Come, you rogue, come, bring me to a
justice.

Host. Ay, come, you starved bloodhound.   30

Doll. Goodman death, goodman bones!

Host. Thou atomy, thou!

Doll. Come, you thin thing! Come, you rascal!

Beadle. Very well.

[Exeunt.]

Scene V. [A street near Westminster Abbey.]

Enter *Grooms,* strewers of rushes.

1. Groom. More rushes, more rushes.

2. Groom. The trumpets have sounded twice.

3. Groom. 'Twill be two o'clock ere they come
from the coronation. Dispatch, dispatch.   *[Exeunt.]*

6. **grace:** honor; **leer upon him:** i.e., give him a knowing look.

11-2. **liveries:** apparel: **bestowed:** spent.

22. **shift me:** change clothing.

28. **semper idem:** always the same; **obsque hoc nihil est:** without this there is nothing.

29. **all in every part:** perfect. Pistol misquotes a proverbial phrase, "All in all, and all in every part."

*Trumpets sound and the King and his Train pass
over the stage.* After them enter *Falstaff,
Shallow, Pistol, Bardolph,* and the *Boy.*

Fal. Stand here by me, Master Robert Shallow; I   5
will make the King do you grace. I will leer upon him
as 'a comes by, and do but mark the countenance that
he will give me.

Pist. God bless thy lungs, good knight.

Fal. Come here, Pistol, stand behind me. O, if I had   10
had time to have made new liveries, I would have bestowed the thousand pound I borrowed of you. But
'tis no matter; this poor show doth better. This doth
infer the zeal I had to see him.

Shal. It doth so.   15

Fal. It shows my earnestness of affection—

Shal. It doth so.

Fal. My devotion—

Shal. It doth, it doth, it doth.

Fal. As it were, to ride day and night, and not to   20
deliberate, not to remember, not to have patience to
shift me—

Shal. It is best, certain.

Fal. But to stand stained with travel, and sweating
with desire to see him, thinking of nothing else, put-   25
ting all affairs else in oblivion, as if there were nothing else to be done but to see him.

Pist. 'Tis *semper idem,* for *obsque hoc nihil est.*
'Tis all in every part.

Shal. 'Tis so, indeed.   30

34. **durance:** imprisonment; **contagious:** pernicious.

36. **mechanical:** vulgar. **Mechanical** was used as both a noun and adjective to describe one who worked with his hand; i.e., one of low estate.

37. **ebon:** dark; **fell:** deadly; **Alecto:** one of the Furies, who wore snakes in their hair.

45. **imp of fame:** scion of a famous house.

47. **vain:** foolish.

55. **surfeit-swelled:** swollen as the result of gluttony.

57. **hence:** henceforward; **grace:** virtue.

Pist. My knight, I will inflame thy noble liver,
And make thee rage.
Thy Doll, and Helen of thy noble thoughts,
Is in base durance and contagious prison,
Haled thither   35
By most mechanical and dirty hand.
Rouse up revenge from ebon den with fell Alecto's
  snake,
For Doll is in. Pistol speaks nought but truth.
 Fal. I will deliver her.   40
 Pist. There roared the sea, and trumpet-clangor
sounds.

 [*The trumpets sound.*] Enter the *King* and his
  Train, [the *Lord Chief Justice* among them].

 Fal. God save thy Grace, King Hal, my royal Hal!
 Pist. The heavens thee guard and keep, most royal
imp of fame!   45
 Fal. God save thee, my sweet boy!
 King. My Lord Chief Justice, speak to that vain
  man.
 Just. Have you your wits? Know you what 'tis you
  speak?   50
 Fal. My king! My Jove! I speak to thee, my heart!
 King. I know thee not, old man. Fall to thy prayers.
How ill white hairs become a fool and jester!
I have long dreamed of such a kind of man,
So surfeit-swelled, so old, and so profane;   55
But, being awaked, I do despise my dream.
Make less thy body hence, and more thy grace.
Leave gormandizing. Know the grave doth gape

71. competence of life: means to live by.

Falstaff and Mistress Quickly.
From the frontispiece of Francis Kirkman, *The Wits; or, Sport upon Sport* (1672).

For thee thrice wider than for other men.
Reply not to me with a fool-born jest. 60
Presume not that I am the thing I was,
For God doth know, so shall the world perceive,
That I have turned away my former self.
So will I those that kept me company.
When thou dost hear I am as I have been, 65
Approach me, and thou shalt be as thou wast,
The tutor and the feeder of my riots.
Till then, I banish thee, on pain of death,
As I have done the rest of my misleaders,
Not to come near our person by ten mile. 70
For competence of life I will allow you,
That lack of means enforce you not to evils;
And, as we hear you do reform yourselves,
We will, according to your strengths and qualities,
Give you advancement. Be it your charge, my lord, 75
To see performed the tenor of our word.
Set on.   [*Exeunt the King and his Train.*]
    Fal. Master Shallow, I owe you a thousand pound.
    Shal. Yea, marry, Sir John, which I beseech you to
let me have home with me. 80
    Fal. That can hardly be, Master Shallow. Do not
you grieve at this. I shall be sent for in private to him.
Look you, he must seem thus to the world. Fear not
your advancements; I will be the man yet that shall
make you great. 85
    Shal. I cannot well perceive how, unless you
should give me your doublet and stuff me out with
straw. I beseech you, good Sir John, let me have five
hundred of my thousand.

91. **color:** pretense.

92. **color:** i.e., collar, or hangman's noose.

93. **colors:** enemy standards. The phrase is proverbial.

95. **soon at night:** tonight; this very night.

96. **Fleet:** Fleet Prison.

105. **conversations:** behaviors.

111. **civil swords:** swords unsheathed for domestic strife.

Fal. Sir, I will be as good as my word. This that 90
you heard was but a color.

Shal. A color that I fear you will die in, Sir John.

Fal. Fear no colors. Go with me to dinner. Come,
Lieutenant Pistol, come, Bardolph. I shall be sent for
soon at night.   95

Enter [*Lord Chief*] *Justice* and *Prince John* [*with
Officers*].

Just. Go, carry Sir John Falstaff to the Fleet.
Take all his company along with him.

Fal. My lord, my lord—

Just. I cannot now speak. I will hear you soon.
Take them away.   100

Pist. *Si fortuna me tormenta, spero contenta.*

Exeunt [*all but Prince John and the Chief Justice*].

John. I like this fair proceeding of the King's.
He hath intent his wonted followers
Shall all be very well provided for,
But all are banished till their conversations   105
Appear more wise and modest to the world.

Just. And so they are.

John. The King hath called his Parliament, my lord.

Just. He hath.

John. I will lay odds that, ere this year expire,   110
We bear our civil swords and native fire
As far as France. I heard a bird so sing,
Whose music, to my thinking, pleased the King.
Come, will you hence?

[*Exeunt.*]

11-12. **like an ill venture it come unluckily home:** i.e., like a merchant ship returning from an unprofitable voyage; **break:** go bankrupt.

14. **Bate me some:** subtract some of my debt.

EPILOGUE

IIIIIIIIIIIIIIIIIIIIIIIIIIIIIIIIIIIIIIIIIIIIIIIIIIIIIIIIIIIIIIIIIIIIIIIIIIIIIIIIIIIIIII

[Spoken by a Dancer]

First my fear; then my curtsy; last my speech. My fear is, your displeasure; my curtsy, my duty; and my speech, to beg your pardons. If you look for a good speech now, you undo me, for what I have to say is of mine own making, and what indeed I should say will, I doubt, prove mine own marring. But to the purpose, and so to the venture. Be it known to you, as it is very well, I was lately here in the end of a displeasing play, to pray your patience for it and to promise you a better. I meant indeed to pay you with this, which, if like an ill venture it come unluckily home, I break, and you, my gentle creditors, lose. Here I promised you I would be and here I commit my body to your mercies. Bate me some and I will pay you some and, as most debtors do, promise you infinitely.

If my tongue cannot entreat you to acquit me, will you command me to use my legs? And yet that were but light payment, to dance out of your debt. But a good conscience will make any possible satisfaction, and so would I. All the gentlewomen here have forgiven me. If the gentlemen will not, then the gentlemen do not agree with the gentlewomen, which was never seen before in such an assembly.

One word more, I beseech you. If you be not too

much cloyed with fat meat, our humble author will
continue the story, with Sir John in it, and make you
merry with fair Katherine of France. Where, for any
thing I know, Falstaff shall die of a sweat, unless
already 'a be killed with your hard opinions, for Old-   30
castle died a martyr, and this is not the man. My
tongue is weary. When my legs are too, I will bid you
good night, and so kneel down before you, but, indeed, to pray for the Queen.

KEY TO

Famous Passages

I am not only witty in myself, but the cause that
   wit is in other men. *[Falstaff—*I. ii. 9-10]

Your lordship, though not clean past your youth, hath
   yet some smack of age in you, some relish of the
   saltness of time. *[Falstaff—*I. ii. 96-98]

It was alway yet the trick of our English nation, if
   they have a good thing, to make it too common. . . . I
   were better to be eaten to death with a rust than to
   be scoured to nothing with perpetual motion.
                                    *[Falstaff—*I. ii. 214-20]

I can get no remedy against this consumption of the
   purse. Borrowing only lingers and lingers it out, but
   the disease is incurable. *[Falstaff—*I. ii. 236-38]

He hath eaten me out of house and home. *[Quickly—*II. i. 74]

Away, you moldy rogue, away! I am meat for your
   master. *[Doll—*II. iv. 125-26]

O sleep, O gentle sleep,
Nature's soft nurse, how have I frighted thee . . . ?
Uneasy lies the head that wears a crown. *[King—*III. i. 5-31]

A man can die but once. We owe God a death. . . .
And let it go which way it will, he that dies
   this year is quit for the next. *[Feeble—*III. ii. 235-39]

I do remember him at Clement's Inn like a man made
   after supper of a cheese paring. When 'a was naked,
   he was for all the world like a forked radish, with
   a head fantastically carved upon it with a knife.
                                    *[Falstaff—*III. ii. 307-11]

Thy wish was father, Harry, to that thought. *[King—*IV. v. 106]